text and
photographs by
Jill Dupleix

quadrille

Jill Dupleix
totallysimplefood

notes

All spoon measures are
level; 1 tsp = 5 ml spoon;
1 tbsp = 15 ml spoon.
All eggs are free-range
and large; all herbs are
fresh; all salt is sea salt,
and all pepper is freshly
ground black pepper
unless otherwise stated.
All recipe ideas serve 4
unless otherwise suggested.

Editorial Director Jane O'Shea
Creative Director Mary Evans
Project Editor Janet Illsley
Design assistant Claire Peters
Editorial assistant Laura Herring
Production Rebecca Short

This edition first published in 2005 by
Quadrille Publishing Limited
Alhambra House
27-31 Charing Cross Road
London WC2H OLS

Reprinted in 2005, 2006
10 9 8 7 6 5 4 3

The material in this book was previously
published in *Simple Food* and
Very Simple Food

Text and photographs
© 2002, 2003, 2005 Jill Dupleix
Design and layout
© 2005 Quadrille Publishing Limited

Cataloguing in Publication Data:
a catalogue record for this book is
available from the British Library.

ISBN-13: 978 184400 167 5
ISBN-10: 1 84400 167 9
Printed in Singapore

www.jilldupleix.com

This is the sort of cookbook you can use every day. The techniques are easy, the tools are basic, and the flavours are strong and natural.

Use it when you have just walked in the door with the same old chicken breast, fish fillet or packet of pasta, and you need a bit of inspiration. Or when you have plenty of inspiration and just want something that you won't grow old cooking. Or when you need something fresh and bright that is healthy enough to keep you out of the clutches of faddy diet and self-help gurus.

I think of it as simple food for complicated people. Like most people who love food, I get my ideas from good, fresh produce in season. If you have great ingredients at their best, there is no need for artificiality and extra work, because the real thing is good enough. Shop well, and it automatically follows that you will cook well and eat well.

I don't make my own pastry, I won't deep-fry, and I can't for the life of me stone olives or peel grapes. I drink while I cook, do the dishes as I go, and am a great believer in cheating in the kitchen, as long as you don't kill anyone.

Life is hard enough as it is, without us turning cooking into a chore instead of a pleasure. That's why we need to keep things simple, for our food and for ourselves.

starters

Cucumber 'sandwiches'

This is a blindingly simple and endlessly flexible idea for all you canapé crusaders out there. Cucumber rounds give you freshness and crunch, and carry all manner of sympathetic flavours, such as smoked salmon (featured here), smoked trout, fresh prawns or crab.

Peel the cucumber lengthwise, leaving a few thin strips of skin for a decorative effect. Cut the cucumber into 1cm slices – you should get around 32 slices.

Arrange half the cucumber slices on a board. Dab a little horseradish sauce on each one to help the salmon stay in one place. Cut the smoked salmon into 16 pieces, fold loosely and arrange on top of the cucumber slices on the board. Season with salt and pepper.

Cover with another cucumber slice. Add a little dab of horseradish sauce and top with a parsley leaf and a salted caper, then serve.

MAKES 16

1 long cucumber

2 tbsp horseradish sauce

150 g thinly sliced smoked
   salmon

sea salt

freshly ground black pepper

16 flat-leaf parsley sprigs

16 salted capers

Lemon mussels

Why serve mussels out of their shells when the shells can double as perfect little appetiser plates? Do this as a big party platter, or as elegant individual first courses.

Discard any broken mussels, and those that do not close when sharply tapped. Scrub the mussels well and pull out the little beards. Put the wine, parsley stems and garlic in a large lidded pan and bring to the boil. Add the mussels, cover with the lid and cook for 1 minute, then shake the pan, remove lid and take out the mussels as they open. Repeat this process, discarding any mussels that don't open.

Let the mussels cool to room temperature, then discard the top half-shells, saving four. Arrange the mussels on platters. Mix the preserved lemon with the parsley, olive oil and lemon juice. Spoon a little lemony dressing onto each mussel in the half-shell.

Beat the mayonnaise with the paprika and spoon into the reserved shells for dipping. Put one on each platter and serve.

SERVES 4
1.5 kg black mussels
250 ml dry white wine
handful of parsley stems
2 garlic cloves, squashed
2 tbsp finely chopped
preserved lemon
2 tbsp finely chopped parsley
2 tbsp extra virgin olive oil
1 tbsp lemon juice
2 tbsp quality mayonnaise
1/2 tsp paprika

11

Chipolata oysters

Cold oysters are great on their own, but they are even better with hot little sausages on the side. Take a bite of a hot, peppery beef chipolata, then slurp down a cold, salty, tangy oyster. Repeat until nothing is left.

Scrub the oysters well. Wrap a good thick tea towel around your left hand and hold an oyster firmly in your palm, the flat side facing upwards, the thin, pointy end towards you. Push the point of the knife firmly through the hinge, feeling your way, twisting the blade slightly and increasing the pressure until you feel it give way.

Wipe the blade free of any grit, and run it neatly under the top shell. Lift off the top shell, but keep the oyster steady so you don't lose its natural juices. Loosen the oyster from its shell and set the shell down on a bed of watercress or parsley. Repeat to open the rest of the oysters.

Lightly oil a non-stick fry pan. Prick the sausages well and pan-fry them gently, turning once or twice. When they are sizzling hot and cooked through, drain them on paper towel and arrange next to the oysters. Add the lime or lemon quarters and serve, with flutes of Champagne or tankards of beer.

SERVES 4
12 large fresh oysters
watercress or parsley sprigs
16 beef chipolata sausages
1 lime or lemon, quartered

Belgian mussels

Mussels are easy. Just wash them well and pull out the little beards, discarding any that don't close when tapped. Serve with crusty bread and a pot of real mayonnaise for dipping.

Give the mussels a quick scrub; pull out the little beards and discard.

Peel the onion and slice into fine rings. Heat the butter and oil in a large lidded pan, and cook the onion gently for 5 minutes.

Add the white wine, chicken stock, celery and garlic cloves, and bring to the boil. Add the mussels, cover with the lid and cook for 1 minute, then shake the pan, remove the lid and take out the mussels that have opened.

Repeat this process a few times, discarding any mussels that refuse to open. Add the cream and parsley to the pan, and gently warm through, stirring.

Distribute the mussels among 4 warmed, deep soup bowls and pour the creamy broth on top.

SERVES 4

1.5 kg mussels

1 onion

1 tbsp butter

1 tbsp olive oil

200 ml dry white wine

250 ml light chicken stock
   or water

2 celery stalks, finely sliced

2 garlic cloves, peeled and
   smashed

2 tbsp pouring cream

2 tbsp chopped parsley

soy roasted nuts

Soy roasted nuts

This simple technique not only freshens up mixed nuts, it coats them with a lightly crunchy, seductively sweet-salty flavour. Tamari is a wheat-free soy sauce, available in Asian stores and helpful supermarkets.

Heat the oven to 180°C/Gas 4. Line the base of a roasting tray with a sheet of foil, scatter the nuts on the foil and roast for 10 minutes, tossing them occasionally.

Mix the tamari and sugar in a bowl. Remove the tray from the oven and tip the nuts into the bowl, tossing until well coated. Using a slotted spoon, return the nuts to the foil-lined tray. Roast for up to 10 minutes until they are dry, tossing every minute or so and watching carefully to ensure they don't burn.

Leave the roasted nuts on the tray until they are completely cool, then store in an airtight jar until needed. Serve with drinks, or scattered through salads.

MAKES 500g

500g mixed shelled nuts
(eg blanched almonds, brazil nuts, hazelnuts, pistachios)

100ml tamari or soy sauce

1 tbsp caster sugar

Smoked salmon martini

Save on making cocktail snacks for your next party, by putting the cocktail snack in the cocktail. First, you sip the vodka martini, then you eat the vodka-marinated smoked salmon and the olive. Then you have another one.

First, chill four martini glasses until they are frosty. Cut the smoked salmon slices in half lengthwise, twist each piece into a spiral and place in the glasses.

Pour the vodka and dry vermouth over ice into a shaker, stir well and strain into the glasses. Add a green olive to each glass and serve.

MAKES 4
2 thin slices smoked salmon
300 ml vodka
60 ml dry vermouth
4 green or stuffed olives

Parmesan biscuits

These rich, cheesy little biscuits make the perfect nibble with drinks. Send out a stack with a tray of icy cold dry martinis, or tall, frosty glasses of chilled white wine, or serve them with little cups of creamy vegetable soup.

Heat the oven to 180°C/Gas 4. Cut the butter into small dice. Put the butter, flour, cheese, sea salt, pepper and cayenne in the food processor and whiz until sandy. Add the iced water and whiz again until the dough is moist and clumpy. Add extra water if necessary.

Form into a ball, roll out to 1 cm thickness on a lightly floured bench, and cut into 5 cm rounds. Place on a non-stick baking tray, brush lightly with beaten egg, and scatter with thyme and rosemary.

Bake for 10 to 12 minutes or until lightly golden, then transfer to a wire rack to cool. Store in an airtight container for up to 2 weeks.

MAKES 12
100g butter, chilled
150g plain flour
80g parmesan, cheddar or
    gruyère, grated
1/2 tsp sea salt
freshly ground black pepper
pinch of cayenne pepper
1 tbsp iced water
1 free-range egg, beaten
1 tbsp thyme and rosemary
    leaves

Thai corn cakes

Crisp, golden little fritters that practically pop in the mouth with juicy corn kernels. Stack high and drizzle with sweet, seedy Thai chilli sauce.

Whiz half the sweetcorn in a blender to a purée. Pound the garlic, shallots and coriander stalks until smashed. Add to the blender with the sugar, fish sauce, salt and pepper, and whiz to a purée.

Add the flour and whiz for 1 minute, then add the eggs and process for another 30 seconds. Tip into a bowl and fold through the remaining sweetcorn, reserving 1 tbsp for serving.

Heat the oil in a heavy-based frying pan until it starts to smoke. Drop 4 tablespoonfuls of batter into the pan, spacing them apart, and cook until golden, turning once. Remove and drain on paper towels. Keep warm while you make the remaining cakes.

Scatter with corn kernels and spring onions, and drizzle with sweet chilli sauce to serve.

MAKES 16

275g canned sweetcorn
kernels, drained
2 garlic cloves, peeled
2 shallots, peeled
2 coriander stalks
1 tsp caster sugar
1 tbsp Thai fish sauce
1 tsp sea salt
1/2 tsp freshly ground
black pepper
100g plain flour
2 large free-range eggs
2 tbsp vegetable oil,
for frying
2 spring onions, finely chopped
100 ml sweet chilli sauce

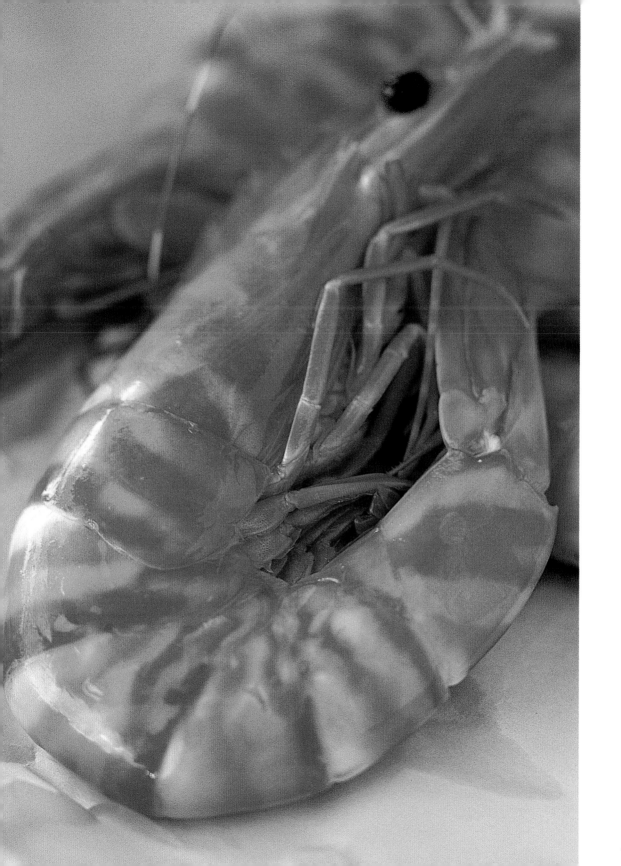

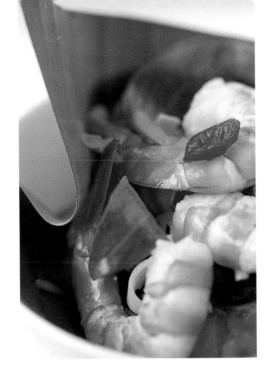

Coconut prawns with chilli

This is fast, simple, and comes with all those tangy tastes you love in Thai food. No time? Then use cooked prawns and add a little coconut milk to the dressing.

Devein the prawns by hooking a thin bamboo skewer through the spine and pulling out the black thread, but don't peel them. Heat the coconut milk, salt and water in a pan until simmering. Add the prawns and simmer for 3 to 4 minutes until they change colour. Remove and cool, then peel, leaving the tail intact.

Trim the lemongrass and finely slice the white section only. Finely slice the chillies and shallots. Cut the kaffir lime leaves (if using) into thin ribbons.

Combine the lemongrass, chillies, shallots, lime leaves or zest, mint and coriander in a bowl. Add the prawns and toss gently. Mix sugar, lime juice, fish sauce and 3 tbsp of the coconut milk and add to the prawns. Toss lightly and serve at room temperature, scattered with crushed peanuts.

SERVES 4

16 medium raw prawns

250 ml canned coconut milk

salt

250 ml water

1 lemongrass stalk

2 small red chillies

4 shallots, peeled

4 kaffir lime leaves, or 1 tsp grated lime zest

handful of mint leaves

handful of coriander leaves

1 tbsp sugar

2 tbsp lime juice

1 tbsp Thai fish sauce (nam pla)

2 tbsp salted peanuts, crushed

party sushi

Party sushi

Make these just before guests arrive and keep in an airtight container, or turn the making of them into a party piece, and keep them rolling out to order. Party, or temaki sushi are light, fresh and healthy, and fun to eat in your hands. Add cooked prawns, sashimi-quality tuna or avocado, as you see fit.

MAKES 20

Sushi rice:

60ml rice vinegar

2 tbsp caster sugar

1 tsp salt

400g sushi rice

500ml water

To assemble:

1/2 cucumber

1 sweet red pepper

1 sweet yellow pepper

2 tsp wasabi powder

1 tbsp quality mayonnaise

20 sheets nori (toasted
    seaweed sheet)

250g thinly sliced smoked
    salmon

To make the sushi rice dressing, gently heat the rice vinegar, sugar and salt in a small pan until the sugar has dissolved, then cool.

Wash the rice in a sieve under cold running water, drain well, tip into a saucepan and add the water. Bring to the boil, cover tightly and simmer very gently for 15 minutes. Turn off the heat and leave for another 10 minutes undisturbed, then turn the rice out onto a baking sheet or tray.

Sprinkle the rice with the cooled dressing, tossing it well with a wooden spoon to cool it quickly. Keep the rice covered with a damp cloth until ready to use, which should be the same day.

Cut the cucumber and sweet peppers into thin batons or strips, discarding the pepper core and seeds. Mix the wasabi powder to a paste with the mayonnaise.

Place a heaped tablespoonful of sushi rice on the left-hand side of a sheet of nori. Add a dab of wasabi mayonnaise, a small fold of smoked salmon, some cucumber, and red and yellow pepper strips, and roll from left to right into a cone shape. A few grains of rice will help the final flap stick. Eat in the hands.

Tuna with sesame soy

Really fresh tuna has a pure, sweet flavour and melt-in-the-mouth texture. This no-cook, no-fuss, first course makes the most of tuna by teaming it with soy sauce, sesame oil and mirin (sweet rice wine), available from Japanese food stores and helpful supermarkets.

Trim the tuna of all bloodlines and cut into a neat shape to enable you to cut it into small dice, around 1cm. Discard any obvious sinews or icky bits.

Whisk the soy sauce, mirin, sesame oil and mustard together in a bowl. Add the tuna and toss lightly to coat in the dressing.

Mix the rice vinegar and olive oil with sea salt and pepper in a second bowl. Pick the leaves from the watercress, toss in the dressing, then arrange on four serving plates.

Pile the tuna in little pyramids on top of the leaves, and scatter with finely snipped chives. Serve with chopsticks.

SERVES 4

350g fresh sashimi-quality tuna
1 tbsp soy sauce
1 tbsp mirin
1 tsp sesame oil
½ tsp Dijon mustard
1 tsp rice vinegar
1 tbsp olive oil
sea salt
freshly ground black pepper
100g watercress
1 tbsp finely snipped chives

Smoked salmon rolls

These glamorous rolls fulfil my three main criteria for easy entertaining: they take only minutes to make; can be done ahead of time; and they look a million dollars. Serve as a sit-down first course, or with drinks.

Beat 1 tbsp horseradish into the mascarpone. Gradually add the rest to taste – until the horseradish cream is hot enough for you. Add the chives, sea salt and pepper and fold them through the cream. (You can make this beforehand and refrigerate it.)

Trim the smoked salmon into 8 strips, each 15 x 5 cm. Place a spoonful of the horseradish cream on one end of each strip and roll up. It doesn't matter if the edges are a bit ragged.

Sit each smoked salmon roll on its end, and scatter extra chives on the exposed cream at the top. (You can even do this an hour or two beforehand and refrigerate until required.) Serve one or two salmon rolls per person.

MAKES 8

2 tbsp hot horseradish sauce

450g mascarpone or crème fraîche

2 tbsp finely snipped chives, plus extra to serve

sea salt

freshly ground black pepper

250g thinly sliced smoked salmon

Salami tarts

I had some leftover pastry and salami, so I did the only thing possible – I made salami tarts, chilled a bottle of Spanish sherry and invited people around for a drink. The softer and fresher the salami – look for a Venetian-style soppressa – the better the tart.

Heat the oven to 200°C/Gas 6. Roll out the pastry thinly. Remove the skin from the salami slices. Place one salami slice on the pastry and cut around it, leaving a 1 cm border of pastry. Use this as your size guide for cutting out 10 identical pastry circles.

Brush each pastry round with beaten egg and top with a slice of salami. Bake for 10 minutes or until the pastry borders are puffy and golden. Transfer to a wire rack – they will crisp as they cool.

To cook the Swiss chard, wash it well and place in a saucepan with just the water clinging to the leaves. Cover and cook over high heat, tossing occasionally, until the leaves wilt and the juices evaporate. Set aside to cool, and squeeze out excess water. Toss in olive oil, with sea salt and lots of pepper.

Serve the salami tarts at room temperature, topped with a little mound of wilted Swiss chard.

MAKES 10
500g ready-rolled frozen
puff pastry, thawed
12 slices salami, around
6cm diameter
1 free-range egg, beaten
200g Swiss chard leaves
(silverbeet)
1 tbsp extra virgin olive oil
sea salt
freshly ground black pepper

Anchoïade toasts

Provençal anchovy paste has a strong and sunny flavour that makes it the perfect appetizer to have on toasted baguette with drinks in the sunshine. It is also delicious on hard-boiled eggs, or drizzled over roasted vegetables.

Using a pestle and mortar, pound the anchovies, tomato purée and garlic until smooth. Add the olive oil, drop by drop to begin with as you continue to pound, until you have a thick paste. Then add the oil by the teaspoonful, until the mixture is smooth and glossy. Beat in the orange juice and some pepper.

SERVES 6 TO 8

24 canned anchovy fillets
  in oil (2 small cans), drained
2 tbsp tomato purée (paste)
2 garlic cloves, peeled
4–5 tbsp extra virgin olive oil
1 tbsp orange juice
freshly ground black pepper
1 baguette

Finely slice the baguette into 20 or so slices, and grill on both sides until dry and golden. (You can do all this in advance.) Spoon a little anchoïade onto each toast to serve.

Spiced quail eggs

Boil 12 quail eggs in simmering water for 3 minutes. Cool in cold water, then peel and trim a slice off one end so they sit up. Dip the pointy end in smoked paprika and top with a flake of sea salt. Serve with drinks.

Tomato and basil bruschetta

Summer cooking is simple. Get up in the morning, do this to a few ripe tomatoes, leave them to infuse and go back to bed. The first course is almost done.

Cut out the cores from the tomatoes and cut a small cross at the base. Dunk them in a pot of boiling water for 20 seconds, then peel off the skins. Cut the tomatoes in half, squeeze out and discard the seeds and juice, and roughly chop the flesh.

Lightly toss the tomatoes in a bowl with the garlic cloves, basil leaves, sea salt, pepper and olive oil. Cover and set aside in a cool place to infuse. Do this an hour or two before you intend to eat.

When ready to serve, grill or toast the bread on both sides. Dip a pastry brush in the tomato marinade and brush each toast. Pile the tomatoes and basil on top, drizzle with the juices, and serve.

SERVES 4

4 ripe, red tomatoes

2 garlic cloves, peeled and
   smashed

1 cup basil leaves

sea salt

freshly ground black pepper

4 tbsp extra virgin olive oil

4 thick slices sourdough bread

Crumbed goat cheese salad

Buy cooked beetroot or, better still, cook your own beforehand, then team with flash-fried crumbed goat cheese for a fast and simple sit-down first course.

Cut the goat cheese into 4 slices, around 1 cm thick. Coat each slice in olive oil, then in the breadcrumbs, and chill until required.

Peel the cooked beetroot by rubbing off the skin. Trim neatly, slice into paper-thin rounds and arrange in an overlapping ring on each dinner plate. Whisk the dressing ingredients together in a bowl. Toss the rocket or spinach leaves lightly in the dressing and arrange in the centre of the beetroot.

Heat a non-stick fry pan, and dry-fry each slice of goat cheese until golden brown, carefully turning once. Gently lift the goat cheese onto the leaves (it may break up, but that's okay). Drizzle any remaining dressing over and around.

SERVES 4

200 g fresh, firm goat cheese
(in a round or log form)
2 tbsp extra virgin olive oil
3 tbsp fine, dry breadcrumbs
4 medium beetroot, cooked
200 g baby rocket or
spinach leaves

Dressing:
2 tbsp extra virgin olive oil
1 tbsp white wine vinegar
1 tbsp finely snipped chives
sea salt
freshly ground black pepper

oatcakes with goat cheese

Gazpacho with cucumber

This isn't so much a cold soup, as a fresh and healthy vegetable smoothie. If you're feeling flash, drop a cooked prawn into each bowl, as a surprise bonus.

Roughly chop the tomatoes, cucumber, peppers, onion and garlic, and combine in a blender.

Cut off the crusts from the bread and discard. Place the bread in a bowl with just enough water to cover, then immediately squeeze out the water and roughly tear the bread into pieces.

Add the bread to the blender with the sherry vinegar, olive oil, Tabasco, sea salt and pepper. Whiz for a minute or two, until smooth. Press through a fine sieve into a bowl, then cover and chill until ready to serve.

Place a prawn (if using) in each chilled cocktail glass or serving bowl, and top with the vegetable gazpacho. Scatter diced sweet pepper and cucumber on top.

SERVES 4

6 ripe tomatoes

1 cucumber, peeled and seeded

2 sweet red peppers, cored and seeded

1 small onion, peeled

1 garlic clove, peeled

3 thick slices sourdough bread

2 tbsp sherry vinegar

2 tbsp extra virgin olive oil

dash of Tabasco

sea salt

freshly ground black pepper

To serve:

4 cooked prawns (optional)

2 tbsp diced sweet red pepper

2 tbsp diced cucumber

Oatcakes with goat cheese

Why make them when you can buy them? Because they're so much better homemade. Top with oven-roasted cherry tomatoes and tangy goat cheese and serve with drinks.

Heat the oven to 180°C/Gas 4. Toss the cherry tomatoes in olive oil and bake for 15 minutes until soft and squidgy. Remove and cool to room temperature.

To make the oatcakes, whiz the oats, flour, butter and salt in a food processor. Add water, 1 tbsp at a time, until the mixture starts to come together.

Push the dough together with your hands, then gently roll or pat it out on a lightly floured surface until 1 cm thick. Cut into 4 or 5 cm rounds with a pastry cutter or upturned liqueur glass. Re-roll the scraps and cut out more rounds.

Place the oatcakes on a non-stick baking sheet and bake for 10 to 12 minutes. Cool on a wire rack and store in an airtight container. Serve topped with a thin slice of goat cheese and a cherry tomato.

MAKES 20

20 cherry tomatoes
1 tbsp extra virgin olive oil
120 g rolled oats
100 g plain flour
80 g butter, softened
1 tsp sea salt
2–4 tbsp cold water
200 g fresh, firm goat cheese
(in a round log)

Sweetcorn shot soup

You won't believe how sweet this is. The trick is making the base stock with the stripped corn cobs, then adding the corn kernels for more flavour. Serve as a first course, or pour into shot glasses and serve as a chic appetizer with drinks.

Peel the outer leaves from the corn cobs, and discard the leaves and those pesky fine strings. Using a sharp knife, shear off the kernels and set aside. Place the corn cobs in a pan, cover with the cold water, add salt and simmer for 30 minutes, then strain, reserving the broth.

Finely chop the onion. Melt the butter in a pan, and cook the onion for 5 minutes. Add the corn kernels and the strained stock and simmer for 15 minutes. Whiz the soup in a blender until smooth, then strain through a fine sieve, pressing the juices through with a wooden spoon.

To serve, gently reheat the soup, whisk in the cream, salt, pepper and nutmeg, and simmer for 2 minutes. Serve hot, warm or chilled. This quantity will fill 4 soup bowls or 10 small shot glasses.

SERVES 4

4 corn cobs

1.5 litres cold water

sea salt

1 onion, peeled

1 tbsp butter

1 tbsp cream

freshly ground black pepper

1/4 tsp ground nutmeg

Tuna and white bean toast

Whiz 400g drained, canned white beans and 200g canned tuna with its oil in a blender. Add 2 anchovy fillets, black pepper and lemon juice and whiz again. Serve on grilled sourdough bread smeared with garlicky olive oil, with black olives and thyme on top.

party

Americano Pour 30 ml Campari Bitter and 15 ml sweet vermouth over ice in a chilled glass and top with soda water. Add a squeeze and a slice of orange. Serve with potato crisps and tiny finger sandwiches of prosciutto.

Anchovy sticks Cut 400 g ready-rolled puff pastry into long sticks and brush with tomato purée. Thinly slice 12 canned anchovy fillets length-wise, arrange on top and brush with oil from the can. Dust with pepper and paprika and bake at 200°C/Gas 6 for 10 minutes. Serve warm.

Coriander orange olives Gently heat 2 tbsp olive oil with 2 finely sliced garlic cloves, 1 finely sliced red chilli, 6 rosemary sprigs, 6 thyme leaves, 2 bay leaves, 1 tbsp grated orange rind, 1 tbsp coriander seeds and 1 tsp fennel seeds. Add 450 g mixed olives, toss well and let cool.

Avocado, chive and lemon dip Whiz the flesh of 1 ripe avocado with 1 crushed garlic clove, 2 tbsp chopped parsley, 1 tbsp snipped chives, 2 tbsp lemon juice, 2 tbsp yoghurt, sea salt and pepper. Chill. Scatter with chives and serve with corn chips, rice crackers, grissini, or flat bread.

Lemon and smoked salmon dip Whiz 60 g smoked salmon with 200 g cream cheese, 100 ml yoghurt, 2 tsp horseradish cream, 1 tbsp lemon juice and lots of black pepper. Scatter with snipped chives or salmon roe, and serve with warm pitta, crispbread or crackers for dipping.

Things to dip Crisp leaves of witlof or cos, corn chips, grissini (crisp bread rusks), asparagus spears, green beans, prawns, celery sticks, cubes of feta cheese on cocktail sticks, flat bread, baby blinis, potato crisps, Japanese rice crackers, Chinese prawn crackers, Scandinavian crispbread.

Prosciutto grissini Wrap thinly sliced prosciutto (or smoked salmon) around one end of a crisp grissini rusk. Plonk the grissini in a tall glass or vase with a few stalks of rosemary, and serve soon after wrapping or the grissini will soften.

Party tapas Buy up big at a Spanish food store, and put together little toasts of jamon (cured ham) with membrillo (quince paste), manchego cheese, roasted sweet red peppers, anchovy fillets, prawns and sizzled slices of chorizo, in any combination. Serve with chilled sherry.

Tuna sticks with lemon soy Find 500g very fresh sashimi-quality tuna and cut into neat 2cm cubes. Pierce each cube with a cocktail stick, and dip the tuna into white sesame seeds or spicy Japanese pepper. Serve with a dipping sauce of 100ml soy sauce and 1 tbsp lemon juice.

Pesto toasts Cut 200g cherry tomatoes in half, and bake at 180°C/ Gas 4 for 20 minutes. Cut white bread into little squares, place in the turned-off oven until crisp. Cool the toasts, top with a spoonful of pesto and an oven-roasted cherry tomato, add sea salt and pepper and serve.

Champagne gelati Drop two scoops of your favourite store-bought gelato (eg lemon, raspberry) into well chilled champagne flutes and top with chilled Champagne – do this very slowly, or it will froth up and over the glass. Serve icy cold.

Beyond the canapé Put all your money into a 2kg wedge of aged Parmigiano Reggiano cheese, surround it with crusty bread, finely shaved celery, olives and anchovies, and let people help themselves.

prosciutto grissini

brunches & lunches

Pitta pockets

This is my very simple version of an Italian snack made with piadina, a soft, unleavened bread from Emiglia-Romana. I use Greek pitta bread instead, stuffing it with prosciutto, rocket and mozzarella, then warming it until the cheese goes gooey.

Heat the oven to 180°C/Gas 4. Toss the rocket leaves in the olive oil with sea salt and pepper. Drain the mozzarella and slice thinly. Cut the sun-dried tomatoes in half.

Cut or tear the pitta breads in half and gently work them open to form pockets. Stuff each pocket with rocket leaves, prosciutto, sun-dried tomatoes and mozzarella, until quite full. If the bread splits at the side, just wrap in foil to keep it together.

MAKES 4

100g rocket leaves

1 tbsp extra virgin olive oil

sea salt

freshly ground black pepper

2 fresh mozzarella bocconcini (balls), each about 125g

4 sun-dried tomatoes in oil

4 pitta breads

8 slices prosciutto

2 tbsp pesto

Place the stuffed pittas on a tray and heat through in the oven for 4 to 5 minutes, or until the cheese melts. (Or you can warm them on a medium-hot barbecue or griddle for just a few minutes, turning once, until the cheese melts.) Don't heat them for too long, or the bread will turn brittle.

Drizzle a generous teaspoonful of pesto into each stuffed pitta and serve two halves to each person.

Greek stack

A new angle on everyone's favourite Greek salad – serve it stacked high on warm pitta bread. If you want something meatier for lunch, add some spiced grilled lamb or a few garlicky sausages to the side.

Discard the outer cos leaves, then cut the lettuce crosswise into 4 thick, chunky rounds. Thickly slice the tomatoes and season with sea salt and pepper. Cut the feta into 4 chunky slices. Halve the anchovy fillets lengthwise.

To make the dressing, whisk the extra virgin olive oil, lemon juice, sea salt and pepper in a bowl. Add the olives and toss to coat.

Gently warm the pitta bread in a warm oven or on the grill, and place on four warmed dinner plates. Top each pitta with a layer of tomatoes, then a round of cos lettuce, followed by the feta, another slice of tomato, and a few onion rings. Top with anchovy strips and spoon the dressing and olives over the lot.

SERVES 4

1 cos (romaine) lettuce
4 ripe tomatoes
sea salt
freshly ground black pepper
400g good feta cheese
4 anchovy fillets
3 tbsp extra virgin olive oil
1 tbsp lemon juice
2 tbsp kalamata or small black olives
4 small pitta breads
1 onion, very finely sliced

Tunisian salad rolls

One of the world's crunchiest, freshest salads. Serve it with lightly warmed pitta bread, or stuff it into the pitta pocket and eat in your hands.

Finely chop the sweet red pepper, discarding the core and seeds. Cut the tomatoes in half, squeeze out and discard the seeds and juice, and finely chop the flesh. Finely chop the radishes, spring onions and hard-boiled eggs.

Combine the red pepper, tomatoes, radishes, spring onions, eggs, capers and tuna in a large bowl.

Whisk the lemon juice, olive oil, sea salt, pepper, coriander and caraway together. Pour this spiced oil over the salad and toss well.

Lightly warm the pitta breads in the oven or under the grill, then cut off the top 1cm. Fill the pitta pockets with the salad and serve.

SERVES 4

1 sweet red pepper

2 tomatoes

2 small radishes

2 spring onions

2 hard-boiled eggs, peeled

1 tbsp tiny capers, rinsed

300g canned tuna
in oil, drained

8 pitta breads

Spiced oil:

2 tsp lemon juice

1 tbsp olive oil

sea salt

freshly ground black pepper

1/2 tsp ground coriander

1/2 tsp ground caraway

French café salad

You can make a different café salad every day – from eggs, potatoes and tuna, or chicken, beans and tomato, or asparagus, avocado and ham – you get the idea.

Heat the oven to 200°C/Gas 6. Cut the tomatoes in half and arrange on a baking tray. Season with sea salt and pepper, drizzle with 1 tbsp olive oil and bake for 20 minutes.

Cook the potatoes and beans in simmering salted water until tender. Drain and cut the potatoes in half. Peel the hard-boiled eggs and cut into quarters.

Heat 1 tbsp olive oil in a non-stick fry pan and sear the tuna steaks for 3 minutes on each side, leaving the inside pink.

To make the dressing, in a large bowl whisk the wine vinegar, olive oil and mustard with sea salt and pepper until thick.

Dress the rocket leaves, potatoes, beans and olives and arrange on dinner plates with the tomatoes and eggs. Cut the tuna into chunks and place on top, with the anchovy fillets.

SERVES 4

4 plum tomatoes

sea salt

freshly ground black pepper

2 tbsp olive oil

8 small potatoes, peeled

250g fine green beans, trimmed

4 hard-boiled eggs

2 fresh tuna steaks, around 300g each, trimmed

200g rocket or spinach leaves

2 tbsp small black olives

4 anchovy fillets, halved

Dressing:

2 tbsp red wine vinegar

4 tbsp extra virgin olive oil

1 tsp Dijon mustard

Figs and baked ricotta

Place 500g fresh ricotta in a baking dish. Scatter with sea salt, pepper, thyme and rosemary, drizzle with extra virgin olive oil and bake at 200°C/Gas 6 for 15 minutes.
Add 6 halved ripe figs and bake for another 10 minutes.
Serve with prosciutto, drizzled with olive oil and balsamic vinegar.

Egyptian beetroot dip

Whiz 5 cooked, peeled beetroot in a blender with 300 ml yoghurt, 2 crushed garlic cloves, 2 tbsp lemon juice, 2 tbsp extra virgin olive oil, sea salt, pepper and ½ tsp each of ground cumin, coriander, paprika and cinnamon. Serve with warm flat bread for dipping.

Haloumi, tomato and beans

Fresh haloumi is a rich, salty Greek-Cypriot cheese sold pre-packed in plastic, with a little brine.

Heat the oven to 180°C/Gas 4. Cut the tomatoes in half lengthwise and arrange in a baking tin. Drizzle with 1 tbsp olive oil, sea salt, pepper and thyme, and bake for 30 minutes until soft.

Cook the green beans in simmering salted water for 5 minutes.

SERVES 4

8 plum tomatoes

2 tbsp olive oil

sea salt

freshly ground black pepper

few thyme sprigs

400g green beans, topped

400g haloumi

1 lemon, quartered

Dressing:

1 tbsp lemon juice

2 tbsp extra virgin olive oil

1 tbsp capers, rinsed

1 tbsp chopped parsley

Rinse the haloumi, then cut into slices, a little less than 1 cm thick. Heat the remaining olive oil in a non-stick fry pan and, when hot, sizzle the haloumi slices until golden brown. Turn briefly and sizzle the other side.

Whisk the lemon juice, olive oil, capers and parsley together. Drain the beans and toss in the dressing. Arrange the tomatoes and beans on 4 dinner plates, and top with haloumi. Drizzle with the dressing and serve, with lemon.

sizzle haloumi until golden

Amish pancakes

Soft, light oatmeal pancakes to stack high with crisp bacon or soft prosciutto, and drizzle with maple syrup.

Heat the milk to just below boiling point, remove from the heat, and add the rolled oats and sugar. Stir well, and leave to cool.

Sift the flour, baking powder and salt together into a large bowl, add the cooled mixture, and stir well. Beat the egg yolks lightly and stir into the mixture.

Beat the egg whites in a dry bowl until stiff and peaky, then lightly fold into the pancake batter.

Grill or pan-fry the bacon rashers (if using) until crisp, and drain on paper towel.

Heat a large non-stick fry pan and add a teaspoon of butter. Drop tablespoons of batter into the pan and cook over medium heat. When bubbles appear on top, turn and cook the other side until golden. Remove and keep warm. Add another teaspoon of butter, and repeat to cook the rest of the pancakes.

Serve 2 or 3 pancakes per person. Stack them with bacon or prosciutto and drizzle with maple syrup.

MAKES 12

400 ml milk

100 g rolled oats

1 tbsp sugar

1 tbsp plain flour

2 tsp baking powder

pinch of salt

2 large free-range eggs, separated

8 thin rashers rindless bacon, or 8 thin slices prosciutto

unsalted butter for frying

maple syrup or golden syrup, to serve

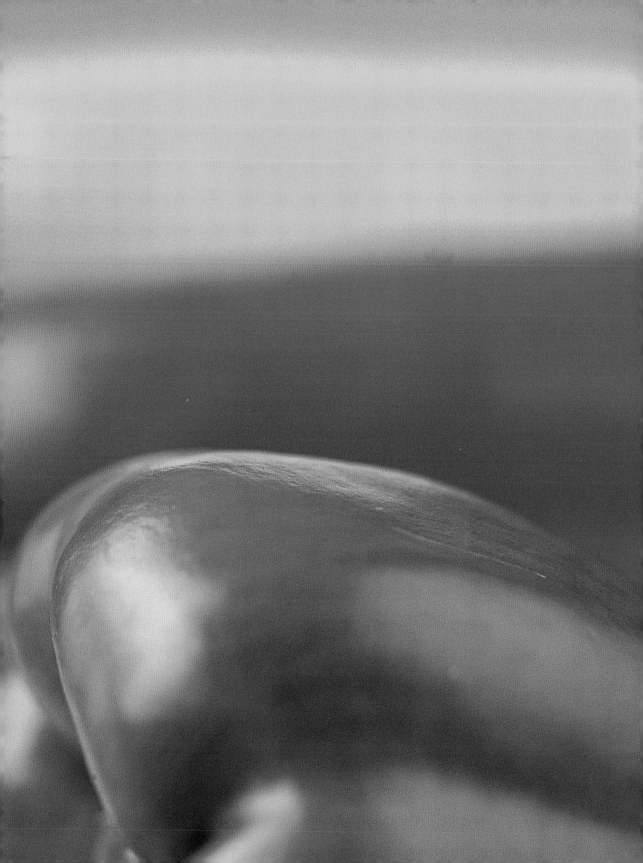

Warm Mediterranean veg

A meal in itself for vegetable lovers, or a simple, colourful accompaniment to fish, sausages, lamb or chicken.

Heat the oven to 180°C/Gas 4. Cut the onion in half and slice finely. Cut the red and yellow peppers into long strips, discarding the core and seeds.

Heat the 1 tbsp oil in a fry pan, and fry the onion and peppers for 10 minutes until they start to soften. Slice the courgettes and tomatoes into rings.

Arrange the onion and peppers in the base of a lightly oiled baking tin or gratin dish, and layer the sliced courgettes and tomatoes on top – in any order you like.

Mix the extra virgin olive oil with the lemon juice, garlic, rosemary, thyme, sea salt and pepper. Drizzle over the vegetables and bake for about 1 hour until tender. Serve hot or warm.

SERVES 4

1 onion, peeled

1 sweet red pepper

1 sweet yellow pepper

1 tbsp olive oil

4 medium courgettes
   (zucchini)

4 Roma tomatoes

2 tbsp extra virgin olive oil

1 tbsp lemon juice

1 garlic clove, peeled and
   crushed

4 rosemary sprigs

6 thyme sprigs

sea salt

freshly ground black pepper

Couscous with dates

Golden couscous makes a light and healthy lunch, with a spicy, fragrant broth and some simple steamed vegetables.

Heat the oven to 160°C/Gas 3. Place the couscous in a large heatproof bowl and pour the boiling water on top. Add the olive oil and diced butter, and toss them through with a fork. Cover and place in the oven for 15 minutes.

Meanwhile, finely slice the onions. Heat the oil in a pan and fry the onions until soft. Add the garlic, tomatoes, sugar, salt, pepper, saffron, paprika, ginger and parsley, and simmer for 10 minutes.

Steam or lightly boil the courgettes, dried apricots and dates for 5 minutes, then drain and thickly slice the courgettes.

Run a fork through the couscous to break up any lumps and season with salt. Pile into warm bowls and top with the courgettes, apricots and dates. Serve, with the hot tomato broth to the side.

SERVES 4
Couscous:
500g couscous
500ml boiling water
1 tbsp olive oil
1 tbsp butter, diced

Vegetables and broth:
2 onions, peeled
2 tbsp olive oil
2 garlic cloves, peeled and crushed
400g canned chopped tomatoes
1 tsp sugar
sea salt
freshly ground black pepper
$\frac{1}{2}$ tsp powdered saffron
1 tsp paprika
1 tsp ground ginger
2 tbsp chopped parsley
6 courgettes (zucchini), green and yellow
12 dried apricots
10 moist, dried dates, pitted and sliced

baked scotch eggs

Salmon egg tarts

This is a sequel to the little ham and egg pies that appeared in Simple Food. Muffin moulds are filled with fresh salmon, cream, curry powder and a whole egg, and baked to produce effortless, pastryless tarts.

Heat the oven to 160°C/Gas 3. Lightly oil or butter a 12-hole muffin tray. Finely chop the raw or cooked salmon and place in a bowl. Add the cream, curry powder, sea salt, pepper, and dill or chives, and mix lightly with a fork.

Divide the salmon mixture between the moulds, then break an egg into each mould. Using a fork, jiggle the egg white so that it mixes with some of the salmon, leaving the yolk whole.

Bake for 20 to 25 minutes until set. Leave to cool for 5 minutes, then run a knife around each mould to loosen, and remove the egg tarts to a wire tray.

Scatter with dill or chives and eat warm or at room temperature. Serve one as a starter with drinks, two with a salad for lunch, or take the lot on a picnic.

MAKES 12
1 tsp olive oil or butter
400 g salmon fillet, raw or
   cooked
2 tbsp single cream
1 tsp curry powder
½ tsp sea salt
freshly ground black pepper
2 tbsp finely chopped dill or
   snipped chives, plus extra
   to serve
12 free-range eggs

Baked Scotch eggs

Because I don't deep-fry, I've invented other ways of having my favourite foods. These Scotch eggs are baked in a muffin tray, in a wrap of bacon. No crumbing, no deep-frying. Simple, really.

Heat the oven to 190°C/Gas 5. Lightly oil a 12-hole muffin tray. Put the eggs in a large pan of hot water, bring to the boil and simmer for 5 minutes from the moment the water starts to bubble. Immediately drain and run under cold water to stop further cooking; cool and peel.

Soak the bread in the milk for 1 minute. Drain and squeeze dry. Combine the bread and sausagemeat in a bowl, using your hands. Add the beaten egg, parsley, nutmeg, salt and pepper and mix well.

Line each muffin mould with a bacon rasher. Press some meat into the base. Add the egg, pointy end up, and pack the meat around and over the egg to cover completely. Bake for 20 minutes until nicely browned. Leave in the moulds for 10 minutes. Drain off any juices, run a knife around to loosen and serve hot, warm or cold.

MAKES 12
1 tsp vegetable oil
12 large free-range eggs
5 slices white sandwich
bread, crusts removed
200 ml milk
1 kg good sausagemeat
(eg veal and pork)
1 free-range egg, beaten
1 tbsp chopped parsley
$1/2$ tsp ground nutmeg
sea salt
freshly ground black pepper
12 rindless rashers streaky
bacon

Little egg and ham pies

Line each mould of a muffin tray with ham, crack an egg into it, add cream and a little grated cheese, and bake. Serve warm for brunch, or take on a picnic.

Heat the oven to 180°C/Gas 4. Lightly oil or butter a 12-hole muffin tray. Line the base and most of the sides of each mould with a slice of ham, then break an egg into the hollow. Drizzle with the cream, and scatter with sea salt, pepper, parsley and parmesan.

Bake for 15 to 20 minutes until the egg is just set and starting to shrink away from the sides of the tin. Leave to cool for 5 minutes, then run a knife around each mould to loosen the ham and egg, and remove to a wire tray. Eat warm, or at room temperature.

MAKES 12

1 tsp olive oil or butter

12 thin slices good quality ham

12 large free-range eggs

2 tbsp cream

sea salt

freshly ground black pepper

2 tbsp roughly chopped parsley

4 tbsp freshly grated parmesan

chicken pies

Chicken pies

Buy a ready-roasted chicken or a Chinatown soy chicken, and these simple, warm chicken pies are even simpler.

Heat the oven to 200°C/Gas 6. Soak the dried mushrooms in hot water to cover for 30 minutes. Strip the meat from the chicken and chop it finely.

Peel and finely chop the shallots. Drain the mushrooms, trim off the stalks and slice the caps finely.

Heat the oil in a pan, and cook the shallots gently until soft. Sprinkle with the flour and cook, stirring, for 2 minutes. Gradually add the chicken stock, stirring. Add the mushrooms, and soy, oyster and hoi sin sauces and simmer for 5 minutes. Remove from the heat, stir in the chicken and coriander, and leave to cool.

Roll out half the pastry and cut into twelve 12 cm squares. Repeat with the other half. Plop 1 tbsp of the chicken mixture on a pastry square, top with another square and press down around the filling to seal. Place a large upturned glass over the top, and trim the pie into a circle. Repeat until all pies are made.

Brush the pies with egg yolk, cut a small slash in the top, and bake for 20 to 25 minutes until golden.

MAKES 12

6 dried shiitake mushrooms

1 medium chicken, roasted
    or poached

4 shallots, or 1 small onion

2 tbsp groundnut or peanut oil

1 tbsp plain flour

250 ml chicken stock

1 tbsp soy sauce

1 tbsp oyster sauce

1 tbsp hoi sin or plum sauce

2 tbsp finely chopped coriander

500 g packet puff pastry

1 egg yolk, beaten with
    1 tbsp milk

Country terrine

A hearty, rustic country pâté to serve with crusty bread, little green cornichons and salad leaves.

Roughly chop the bacon, reserving 4 rashers for the top. Clean and trim the chicken livers, and roughly chop.

Combine the minced pork, bacon and chicken livers in a large bowl, along with the chopped herbs, shallots, garlic, salt, pepper, nutmeg and brandy. Mix well with your hands, then cover and leave in the refrigerator overnight.

Heat the oven to 180°C/Gas 4. Mix the egg into the meat and pile the mixture into a 1 litre ovenproof dish. Shape the top into a mound and cover with remaining bacon. Cover with a tight-fitting lid or foil, and bake for 1½ hours, or until the pâté starts to shrink away from the sides of the dish. Cool slightly, then drain off some of the fat. Serve at room temperature, topped with thyme sprigs.

SERVES 8

200g rindless streaky bacon,
plus 4 extra rashers
250g chicken livers
1kg coarsely minced fatty pork
1 tbsp finely chopped parsley
1 tbsp finely chopped thyme
1 tbsp finely chopped sage
2 shallots, peeled and
finely sliced
2 garlic cloves, peeled
and crushed
2 tsp salt
½ tsp freshly ground
black pepper
½ tsp freshly grated nutmeg
2 tbsp brandy or port
1 large free-range egg, beaten
thyme sprigs, to serve

Honey soy quail

Although it is baked in the oven, this crisp-skinned quail tastes as if it has been barbecued over hot coals in Chinatown, which is exactly how you want it to taste.

Wash the quail and pat dry. Tuck the wing tips in behind the body, and tie the legs together with string. Mix the honey and soy sauce in a bowl, add the quail and coat well. Leave to marinate for 30 minutes. Mix the five-spice powder with the salt and set aside.

Heat the oven to 200°C/Gas 6. Drain the quail, place in a baking tin and drizzle with the sesame oil. Bake the quail for 30 minutes, turning them around once or twice, until the meat is cooked and the skin is crisp and browned.

Serve on a bed of wilted spring onions or spinach, or with the sesame mangetout (snow peas) on page 146. Sprinkle with the five-spiced salt and serve with sweet chilli sauce.

SERVES 4

4 fresh quail, around
200g each
2 tbsp honey
3 tbsp soy sauce
1 tsp five-spice powder
1 tsp salt
1 tsp sesame oil
2 tbsp sweet, seedy Thai
chilli sauce

Parmesan lamb cutlets

I've always loved crumbed lamb cutlets, either hot with mashed potato and peas, or cold on a picnic with a spicy tomato relish. These cutlets have a cheese crumb that makes them even nicer.

Flatten the meat with a meat mallet, leaving it on the bone. Put the flour, salt and pepper in a plastic bag, and toss each chop in the flour, shaking off any excess.

Place the eggs in a shallow bowl, and mix the parmesan and breadcrumbs together in another one.

Heat the oil and butter in a large heavy-based fry pan. Dip each chop in the beaten egg, then in the parmesan crumbs to coat, and fry over medium heat on both sides until crisp and golden brown.

Drain the crumbed cutlets on paper towel. Serve with lemon, and a sharply dressed green salad.

SERVES 4

12 lamb cutlets, well trimmed

2 tbsp plain flour

sea salt

freshly ground black pepper

2 free-range eggs, beaten

2 tbsp finely grated parmesan

4 tbsp dried breadcrumbs

2 tbsp light olive oil

1 tbsp butter

1 lemon, quartered

Mixed grill

When I was growing up in Australia, a mixed grill was the best pub lunch around. This is a bit classier, but just as good.

Cut the steak into 4 pieces. Prick the sausages, and cut bacon rashers in half. Heat a ridged cast-iron grill pan or barbecue.

Cut the courgettes on the diagonal into 1cm slices. Cut the tomatoes in half lengthwise. Brush the courgettes and tomatoes with olive oil and grill or barbecue until soft.

Brush the sausages with olive oil and grill until browned. Fry the bacon in a non-stick fry pan until crisp. Brush the steaks with olive oil and grill for around 3 minutes on one side, then 1 minute on the other, depending on thickness.

Wash the spinach and shake dry. Whisk the olive oil, vinegar, mustard, sea salt and pepper together until thick, dress the leaves and arrange on plates. Top with the grilled vegetables and meats.

SERVES 4

300g beef fillet (eg Scotch),
3cm thick
12 short, spicy beef chipolata sausages
4 thin rashers rindless bacon
2 courgettes (zucchini)
4 plum tomatoes
1 tbsp olive oil
100g baby spinach leaves

Dressing:
2 tbsp extra virgin olive oil
1 tbsp red wine vinegar
1 tsp Dijon mustard
sea salt
freshly ground black pepper

beetroot burgers

spanish meatballs

Beetroot burgers

Australians love beetroot with their burgers, but this idea is actually from Sweden, where beetroot is added to the meat to give it a sweet tang.

Finely chop the onion. Heat the butter and olive oil in a fry pan and cook the onion slowly until pale and soft, then cool.

Combine the minced beef, egg yolks, capers, sea salt and pepper in a bowl, add the onion and mix together thoroughly. Add the pickled beetroot and juice, and mix well. With wet hands, shape the mixture into 4 large, flat burgers (the traditional method) or make 8 smaller, taller patties.

Heat a ridged cast-iron grill pan, oil it and the burgers lightly, and cook them on a medium heat for about 5 minutes each side. (Alternatively heat a little olive oil in a fry pan and cook the burgers over medium heat until brown on each side.)

Meanwhile, toast the muffins. Serve the burgers in the toasted muffins, with a little salad of green leaves, or with wilted spinach and small boiled potatoes.

SERVES 4

1 onion, peeled

1 tbsp butter

1 tbsp olive oil

500g minced beef

2 egg yolks

1 tbsp capers, rinsed and
   chopped

sea salt

freshly ground black pepper

3 tbsp pickled beetroot,
   finely chopped

1 tbsp pickled beetroot juice

4 English muffins

Spanish meatballs

Do this ahead of time and serve as a lazy, light lunch with some salad and the Catalan tomato bread on page 97.

Trim off the crusts and soak the bread in the milk for 5 minutes, then squeeze dry. Using your hands, mix the bread with the meat, garlic, nutmeg, parsley, egg, salt and pepper. Form the mixture into small balls, the size of a walnut, and roll in the flour.

Chop the onion. Cut the green pepper into strips, discarding the seeds.

Heat the olive oil in a heavy-based fry pan, and cook the meatballs in batches until well browned on all sides. Remove and add a little extra oil to the pan. Add the onion and green pepper and cook, stirring, for 5 minutes.

Return the meatballs to the pan, and add the chopped tomatoes, green olives, salt, pepper, sherry and stock. Bring to the boil, then simmer for 30 to 45 minutes until the sauce has reduced and thickened to a sludge. Serve hot.

MAKES 30

2 thick slices stale bread

125ml milk

500g minced lamb or beef

1 garlic clove, peeled and crushed

1/2 tsp freshly grated nutmeg

1 tbsp finely chopped parsley

1 free-range egg

sea salt

freshly ground black pepper

2 tbsp plain flour

1 onion, peeled

1/2 sweet green pepper

2 tbsp olive oil

800g canned chopped tomatoes

12 green Spanish olives

3 tbsp dry sherry

250ml chicken stock

Lamb steak sandwich

This is even nicer than the more traditional steak sandwich, as lamb teams with sweetly caramelised onions for a hearty weekend lunch.

Heat the oven to 180°C/Gas 4. Finely slice the onions and toss in a roasting pan with 2 tbsp olive oil, the balsamic vinegar, salt and pepper. Bake for 30 to 40 minutes until caramelised.

Flatten each lamb fillet or steak with a meat mallet, then cut in two. Combine the extra virgin olive oil, white wine, garlic and oregano in a shallow dish, add the lamb and coat well.

Slice the tomatoes and season with salt and pepper. Beat the mustard into the mayonnaise.

Lightly oil a non-stick fry pan and heat. When it is very hot, add the lamb and sear until crusty, turning once. This will only take a minute or two either side. Season well, and set aside while you toast or grill the bread.

Spread 4 toast slices with the mustard mayonnaise, and arrange the rocket leaves, tomatoes, lamb and caramelised onions on top. Top with the remaining toast slices.

SERVES 4

3 white onions

2 tbsp olive oil

2 tbsp balsamic vinegar

sea salt

freshly ground black pepper

4 lamb fillets or boneless leg steaks, around 180g each

2 tbsp extra virgin olive oil

2 tbsp white wine

1 garlic clove, smashed

1 tbsp oregano leaves

4 vine-ripened tomatoes

1 tbsp Dijon mustard

200g good mayonnaise

8 thick slices sourdough or light rye bread

200g baby rocket leaves

paprika salmon

Chilli lime chicken wings

Thai flavours – garlic, lime juice, coriander and chilli – give chicken wings a boost, turning them into an easy lunch. Serve with a sweet, sticky chilli and lime dipping sauce.

Cut off the tips of the chicken wings, and bend each wing until you can cut cleanly between the joints.

SERVES 4

8 medium chicken wings

4 coriander stalks

4 garlic cloves

1 small red or green chilli

1 tsp salt

1 tsp caster sugar

2 tbsp Thai fish sauce or
   soy sauce

2 tbsp lime juice

2 tbsp vegetable oil

Chilli lime sauce:

100 g sugar

125 ml white vinegar

1 small red chilli, sliced

2 tbsp lime juice

2 tbsp Thai fish sauce

2 tbsp coriander leaves

To serve:
lime quarters

Roughly chop the coriander stalks and pound with the garlic, chilli, salt and sugar until you have a rough paste. Add the fish sauce, lime juice and oil, and stir well. Rub this marinade all over the chicken pieces and leave to marinate in the refrigerator for a couple of hours or overnight, turning once or twice.

Heat the oven to 220°C/Gas 7. Place the chicken on a foil-lined roasting tray and bake for 30 minutes until crisp and golden. Or grill on a ribbed cast-iron griddle or a barbecue, turning once.

To make the chilli lime sauce, heat the sugar, vinegar and sliced chilli in a saucepan, stirring until the sugar has dissolved. Bring to the boil and allow to bubble and reduce for a few minutes until the sauce is syrupy. Remove from the heat and add the lime juice, fish sauce and coriander leaves.

Drizzle the chicken wings with the chilli lime sauce and serve with lime quarters.

Paprika salmon

This is a smart way of cooking salmon for a special lunch, spiking it with paprika oil and serving it simply, with roasted red peppers, capers and watercress.

Heat the oven to 220°C/Gas 7. Lightly oil the peppers and roast for 20 minutes until scorched. Transfer the peppers to a bowl, cover and set aside. Place a good, solid baking tray in the oven to heat up for 3 minutes.

Mix the olive oil with the paprika, sea salt and pepper, and coat the salmon with the spiced oil. Lightly oil the hot baking tray and place the salmon on it, skin-side down. Bake for 10 to 12 minutes, or until the salmon is still a little pink inside.

When the peppers are cool enough to handle, strip off the skin and cut the flesh into strips, discarding the core and seeds. Rinse the watercress, shake dry and discard the thicker stems.

To make the dressing, whisk the ingredients together, with salt and pepper, until slightly thickened. Toss the watercress in the dressing and place on warmed dinner plates. Lay the seared salmon, skin-side up, on the cress and arrange the peppers and capers on top.

SERVES 4

2 sweet red peppers

2 tbsp extra virgin olive oil, plus extra to oil peppers

1 tsp paprika

sea salt

freshly ground black pepper

6 thick salmon fillets, around 200g each

250g watercress

1 tbsp small capers, rinsed

Dressing:

2 tbsp extra virgin olive oil

1 tbsp lemon juice or red wine vinegar

1 tsp caster sugar

Fish in a bag

When you cook fish in a sealed foil bag, it retains all its delicacy and flavour. Add cherry tomatoes, spinach – or fine green beans or asparagus – and garlic to the bag and you get a complete meal with no mess, no fuss, and no loss of flavour.

Wash the spinach leaves well, rinse and shake dry. Heat the oven to 220°C/Gas 7. Cut out four 38cm squares of foil.

Divide the spinach leaves between the foil squares. Season the fish well with sea salt and pepper and place on the spinach. Toss the cherry tomatoes and garlic with the olive oil, salt and pepper, then spoon on top of the fish.

Bring two opposite sides of foil up to meet in the middle, and crimp tightly from the middle to the outer edge, shaping it into a half-moon as you go. Now fold the crimped edge over again, squeezing it tightly so air cannot escape. Bake for 15 minutes until the bag has puffed up like a balloon.

Snip open each parcel, drain off most of the juices, and slide the contents onto warm dinner plates. Drizzle with olive oil and serve with lemon wedges.

SERVES 4
250g spinach leaves
(grown-up, not baby)
4 thick white fish fillets
(eg cod, haddock,
snapper), each 180g
sea salt
freshly ground black pepper
200g cherry tomatoes
2 garlic cloves, thinly sliced
2 tbsp extra virgin olive oil,
plus extra to drizzle
1 lemon, quartered

Salt-grilled sardines

Long after the holiday bills have been paid and the suntan has faded, you can relive the memories of meals eaten by the sea or under the grapevines. These sardines take me right back to the smoky al fresco barbecues of the old Alfama district of Lisbon. And to think some people force themselves to eat oil-rich sardines and mackerel purely for their health.

Coat the sweet peppers with some of the olive oil and grill, turning occasionally, until scorched and blistered all over. Peel off the skin and cut the peppers into long strips, discarding the core and seeds.

Brush the sardines and the grill with oil to help prevent sticking. Roll the sardines in the sea salt, pepper and cayenne.

SERVES 4

2 sweet red peppers

2 tbsp olive oil

8 large or 12 medium sardines, gutted, cleaned and scaled

1 tsp flaked sea salt (eg Maldon)

½ tsp freshly ground black pepper

pinch of cayenne pepper

a little extra virgin olive oil

1 lemon, quartered

Grill or barbecue lightly on one side, then turn the sardines while they are still firm enough to be moved without breaking up. Grill or barbecue on the other side until the skin is scorched and bubbling.

Arrange the grilled sardines and peppers on serving plates. Add a drizzle of extra virgin olive oil and serve with a wedge of lemon.

Sweet onion crostini

If brunch is half breakfast, half lunch – and better than both – then this sweet, slow-cooked onion with Italian prosciutto on hot toast is perfect brunch material. You can use Spanish jamón serrano if you prefer.

Peel the onions and slice finely into rings. Melt the butter with the oil in a heavy-based fry pan, add the onions, sea salt, pepper and rosemary and cook gently for 20 minutes, tossing occasionally, until soft and translucent.

Turn up the heat, add the white wine, and allow it to bubble and reduce, stirring well. Lower the heat and cook for a further 10 to 15 minutes until the onions are soft and gooey. Add the wine vinegar, and toss well. You can leave the onions as they are, which I prefer, or purée them in a food processor and reheat the purée.

SERVES 4

4 large white onions

1 tbsp butter

1 tbsp olive oil

sea salt

freshly ground black pepper

2 rosemary sprigs

250ml white wine

1 tbsp red wine vinegar

4 thick slices sourdough bread

8 thin slices prosciutto

4 rosemary sprigs, to serve

Toast or grill the bread on both sides. Pile a generous amount of sweet onions on the toast and top with folded slices of prosciutto. Tuck in the rosemary sprigs and serve.

Catalan tomato bread

Cut 4 big soft bread rolls in half and lightly grill. Brush with olive oil and rub with a cut garlic clove. Halve 4 ripe tomatoes and rub over the rolls, squeezing the juices and seeds into the bread. Grill until browned, and serve with egg dishes, cured meats and cheeses.

bread

Cherry tomato bruschetta Toss 200g cherry tomatoes in 1 tbsp olive oil and bake at 180°C/Gas 4 for 20 minutes. Smash some garlic cloves in extra virgin olive oil, with sea salt and pepper. Grill 4 thick slices of sourdough bread, brush with the oil and top with the cherry tomatoes. Drizzle with more garlicky olive oil and serve.

Crostini with anchovies and capers Mash 8 canned anchovy fillets in oil with 1 tbsp rinsed capers, 1 tbsp finely chopped parsley and pepper. Mix to a paste, adding oil from the anchovy can, and spread on 2 big slices of grilled sourdough bread. Heat under the grill, then cut into fingers.

Turn soup into zuppa Grill thick slices of sourdough bread, brush with garlicky olive oil and place one slice in each bowl. Pour a simple vegetable and bean soup on top and serve. Try it scattered with grated cheese, too.

Cheat's pizza Spread 4 pitta, naan or Turkish flat breads with tomato salsa. Top with torn bocconcini (mozzarella balls), halved cherry tomatoes, anchovy fillets and dried oregano. Drizzle with extra virgin olive oil and bake at 180°C/Gas 4 for 8 minutes, or heat under the grill.

Crumbs! Mix 3 tbsp fresh breadcrumbs with 1 tbsp butter, 1 tsp lemon juice, $1/2$ tsp ground cumin, salt and pepper. Spoon onto mussels, oysters or sardines before grilling, or spread on fish or chicken fillets before roasting.

Little marmalade toasts Beat 200g mascarpone with 1 tbsp caster sugar, 1 tbsp bitter orange marmalade, and 1 tbsp Cointreau or whisky. Finely slice a baguette and grill lightly on both sides. Spread with a little marmalade, and top with the marmalade mascarpone. Serve with espresso coffee at a brunch party, or after dinner.

Peach bruschetta Cut a dry baguette into two 15cm long sections, split in half lengthwise, and lightly butter. Crush the flesh of 4 ripe peaches or 8 apricots onto the bread, scatter with raspberries and sprinkle with 1 tbsp caster sugar. Bake at 180°C/Gas 4 for 10 to 15 minutes until the bread is crisp. Dust with icing sugar and serve as a dessert with crème fraîche.

Baked feta bread Slash a long baguette (as for garlic bread). Crush 2 garlic cloves in 2 tbsp olive oil with a few rosemary sprigs. Cut 200g feta cheese into slices, coat in the oil and wedge into each cut. Wrap in foil and bake at 180°C/Gas 4 for 10 minutes until hot.

Prosciutto croissants Cut 4 large croissants in half, and lightly grill the cut sides. Cover with sliced prosciutto and top with sliced bocconcini (mozzarella balls). Grill briefly until the cheese is soft, and serve hot.

Italian bread salad Grill 2 thick slices of country style bread and cut into cubes. Combine with 1 finely chopped red pepper, 1 tbsp rinsed capers, 1 crushed garlic clove, 2 anchovy fillets, 1 tbsp black olives, 2 tbsp red wine vinegar and 3 tbsp extra virgin olive oil, and toss.

Avocado and lime toast Crush the flesh of 1 ripe avocado with a pinch of sea salt and a big squeeze of lime juice. Grill 2 thick slices of sourdough bread and brush with garlicky olive oil. Spread the avocado thickly on top and add plenty of black pepper. A brilliant breakfast for two.

Pain perdu au chocolat Make a batter by beating 2 eggs with 2 tbsp caster sugar, 100ml milk and 1 tsp cinnamon. Dip 4 thick slices of stale ciabatta bread in the batter and fry in 1 tbsp butter until golden and crisp. Drizzle with hot chocolate sauce or dip into mugs of hot chocolate.

peach bruschetta

salads & vegetables

Carrot and orange salad

A crisp, refreshing salad, this glows with warm, sweet spices and almost fluorescent sunny colours. It's perfect for a warm day, when you can scatter sliced summer radishes over the top. It's also perfect for a cold day, when it brings sunshine and the bite of winter's oranges to a meal of grilled fish, chicken or lamb.

SERVES 6

450g carrots

1 orange

handful of coriander and mint
  leaves

Dressing:

2 tbsp orange juice

1 tbsp lemon juice

2 tbsp extra virgin olive oil

sea salt

freshly ground black pepper

$\frac{1}{2}$ tsp ground cumin

$\frac{1}{2}$ tsp ground cinnamon

1 tsp icing sugar

Peel the carrots and grate them coarsely. Peel the orange with a knife, removing all white pith. Cut it crosswise into 1 cm thick slices, then into small segments.

Whisk the dressing ingredients together in a large bowl. Add the grated carrot, orange segments, and coriander and mint leaves. Toss lightly to serve.

Bacon and tomato salad

This could be too simple for some, but I love putting fresh salads centre stage and making a meal of them. That way, I can eat my favourite foods, such as crisp bacon, without going overboard on them. Turn this salad into a meal with some pan-fried haloumi cheese, chicken livers, or one of Terry's fried eggs (page 276).

To make the dressing, combine the olive oil, vinegar, mustard, sea salt and pepper in a large bowl and whisk well until combined. Cut half of the cherry tomatoes in half and marinate in the dressing.

Grill the bacon under a preheated grill on both sides until crisp. Drain on paper towels and cut into thick batons.

Wash and spin the leaves dry, then toss in the dressing with the marinated tomatoes and the whole tomatoes. Add the bacon and toss lightly, then distribute among four dinner plates and serve.

SERVES 4
200g cherry tomatoes
4 rashers streaky bacon
200g wild rocket or other
salad leaves

Dressing:
2 tbsp extra virgin olive oil
1 tbsp red wine vinegar
1 tsp Dijon mustard
sea salt
freshly ground black pepper

feta tomato salad

Feta tomato salad

Turn a block of creamy feta cheese into food for the gods with a Greek chorus of chilli, olives, herbs and good olive oil. Serve with drinks, scatter over salads, take on picnics, or serve alongside a lazy al fresco lunch.

Finely slice the chilli into rings and place in a bowl with the olives, rosemary and oregano. Add the olive oil and pepper and stir to combine. (You won't need salt, as feta is quite salty.)

Rinse the feta, pat dry and place in a dish. Pour the marinade on top, cover and leave overnight, or at least for a few hours.

Lift the feta out of the marinade and arrange on a serving plate in its original blocks, or cut into bite-sized cubes. Cut the tomatoes in half, add to the marinade to coat lightly, then spoon over the feta. Serve with crusty bread.

SERVES 4 TO 6

1 small red chilli

2 tbsp kalamata olives

5 rosemary sprigs

1 tsp dried oregano

125 ml extra virgin olive oil

freshly ground black pepper

400 g good feta cheese

200 g cherry or baby plum
tomatoes

Warm spring salad

A fresh, light, warm salad that fills the kitchen with spring-like aromas. Use fresh peas and broad beans in season, or frozen ones out of season – they're perfectly acceptable.

Cook the potatoes in simmering salted water for about 15 minutes until tender. Cook the peas, broad beans and green beans in a separate pan of simmering salted water (with the shallots to make peeling easier) until tender, about 5 minutes. Drain, refresh in cold water and set aside. Pick out the shallots, peel and finely slice.

Heat half the olive oil in a fry pan and gently cook the shallots for 2 minutes. Add the peas and beans and toss to heat through. Drain the potatoes, cut in half on the diagonal and add to the pan. Take off the heat, add remaining olive oil, vinegar, salt and pepper, and toss well.

Scatter the rocket on four warmed plates and top with the beans, peas and potatoes. Drizzle with any remaining dressing and serve.

SERVES 4
12 waxy potatoes (eg kipfler, pink fir apple)
sea salt
450g fresh peas, podded
450g fresh broad beans, podded
250g fine green beans, trimmed
3 shallots (small, red onions)
3 tbsp extra virgin olive oil
2 tbsp red wine vinegar
freshly ground black pepper
150g baby rocket leaves or cress

Warm lentil salad

The great thing about these lentils and their pushy little tomato and mint dressing is that they go with anything. Serve them as a salad, as a meal with a fried egg on top, or with roast chicken. The best lentils are the slate-green French 'lentilles de Puy', available from good food stores.

Rinse the lentils and place in a saucepan with the onion, garlic, bay leaves and 1 litre cold water. Bring to the boil, then reduce the heat and simmer gently for 20 minutes or until the lentils are just tender. Drain thoroughly.

To make the dressing, cut the tomatoes in half, discard the juice and seeds, then chop the flesh. In a bowl, combine the chopped tomato with the mint, parsley, sea salt, pepper, extra virgin olive oil and red wine vinegar.

Toss the still-warm drained lentils in the tomato dressing, and divide between four salad plates. Serve warm.

SERVES 4

250g green or brown lentils

1 onion, finely chopped

2 garlic cloves, smashed

2 bay leaves

Dressing:

2 tomatoes

2 tbsp chopped mint

1 tbsp roughly chopped
   flat-leaf parsley

sea salt

freshly ground black pepper

2 tbsp extra virgin olive oil

1 tbsp red wine vinegar

Fattoush

This crunchy Syrian salad combines crisp grilled bread with fresh, juicy, summery flavours. It's startlingly good with prawns, lobster or crab.

Heat the grill. Open up the flat bread until you have two rounds, and grill lightly until crisp and golden. Crumble into small shards with your hands, and set aside.

Peel the cucumbers, cut in half lengthwise, and scoop out and discard the seeds. Halve the tomatoes and scoop out the seeds and juice. Chop the cucumbers, tomatoes, sweet pepper, radishes and spring onions, and mix with the parsley and mint.

Whisk the olive oil, lemon juice, cinnamon, sea salt and pepper together. Toss the salad in the dressing, add the crisp bread and toss again. Using a slotted spoon, divide the salad between 4 individual plates, or pile onto one big platter.

SERVES 4

1 round of Lebanese flat bread, or 2 pitta breads

2 small Lebanese cucumbers

2 ripe tomatoes

1/2 sweet red pepper

4 small radishes

6 spring onions

3 tbsp finely chopped parsley

3 tbsp finely chopped mint

Dressing:

4 tbsp olive oil

3 tbsp lemon juice

1/2 tsp ground cinnamon

sea salt

freshly ground black pepper

Fig and radicchio salad

When figs are in season, I keep trying to find new ways of eating them so that I can fit more in. This salad combines the rich, warm colours of ripe purple figs, pink prosciutto and ruby-toned radicchio leaves with the crunch of fennel and freshness of mint.

Separate the radicchio leaves, then tear each one roughly in two or three. Very finely slice the fennel bulb crosswise. Quarter the figs.

In a large bowl, whisk the dressing ingredients together. Lightly toss the radicchio leaves, sliced fennel and mint leaves in the dressing, then arrange on four dinner plates.

Arrange the figs on top, and tuck in the slices of prosciutto. Roughly chop or pinch the cheese into sections and scatter over the top. Drizzle any remaining dressing over the salad and serve, with Italian grissini (rusks) or crusty bread.

SERVES 4

2 heads radicchio, trimmed

1 fennel bulb, trimmed

4 ripe figs

20 mint leaves

8 thin slices prosciutto

150g fresh ricotta or goat cheese

Dressing:

2 tbsp extra virgin olive oil

1 tbsp balsamic vinegar

1 tsp cold water

sea salt

freshly ground black pepper

Spanish café salad

Every country with a café culture does a great café salad – a loose, casual combination of readily available produce. This is my idea of a Spanish café salad, using Spain's beautiful serrano ham. It's extremely flexible – you could use prosciutto instead of jamon, add some fresh goat cheese, or drop the artichoke hearts to make it your own.

SERVES 4

150g fine green beans, trimmed

250g asparagus, trimmed

salt

2 tomatoes

½ cucumber

200g mixed salad leaves (eg little gem or baby cos lettuce, rocket, frisée)

8 small artichoke hearts, preserved in oil

2 tbsp olives

12 thin slices serrano ham (jamon)

Dressing:

2 tbsp extra virgin olive oil

1 tbsp sherry or red wine vinegar

sea salt

freshly ground black pepper

Cook the green beans and asparagus in simmering salted water for 4 minutes. Drain and cool under cold running water, then drain again.

Cut the tomatoes into quarters, or eighths if large. Peel the cucumber, halve lengthwise and slice finely.

To make the dressing, whisk the ingredients together in a large bowl. Toss the leaves, green beans and asparagus in the dressing and arrange on four dinner plates. Toss the tomatoes, cucumber, artichoke hearts and olives in any remaining dressing and scatter them freely over the leaves.

Using a fork, pull a few of the buried leaves to the surface. Drape the slices of serrano ham on top of the salad and serve.

japanese salmon with mirin

Japanese salmon with mirin

A light, fresh, tangy salad that's as cool as a cucumber on a warm summer's day or evening. If you think there are too many combinations of salmon and cucumber in this book, you're probably right, but I find the two irresistible.

Score the skin of the cucumber lengthwise with the tines of a fork, then slice finely. Combine the lime or lemon juice, rice vinegar, mirin, sea salt, pepper, sugar and chives in a bowl and stir until the sugar has dissolved. Add the cucumber slices, toss to coat and set aside until ready to serve.

Heat the oil in a non-stick fry pan and sear the salmon fillets on both sides until almost cooked through, but still pink in the centre. Allow to cool, then divide into bite-sized flakes with your fingers.

Drain the cucumber slices, reserving the liquid. Arrange in small mounds on four dinner plates and top with the flaked salmon. Whisk the olive oil with 2 tbsp of the cucumber dressing, salt and pepper, and spoon over and around the salmon.

SERVES 4

1 cucumber

1 tbsp lime or lemon juice

1 tbsp rice vinegar

1 tbsp mirin (Japanese rice wine)

sea salt

freshly ground black pepper

1 tsp caster sugar

2 tbsp finely snipped chives

1 tbsp vegetable oil

450 g fresh salmon fillets

2 tbsp olive oil

Chicken Waldorf

The real reason I lightened up the famous salad of apple, celery and walnuts from The Waldorf Astoria in New York is so I can eat more of it. Do this when you have a crowd to feed for Sunday lunch.

Rinse the chicken and place in a wide, shallow pan. Cover with cold water, add the bay leaf and onion half, and bring to just below the boil. Skim off any froth, and simmer gently for 15 minutes, then cover, turn off the heat and leave to steep for 30 minutes. Drain and allow to cool. (You can prepare to this point in advance, although the chicken will be nicer if it isn't refrigerated.)

To make the dressing, whisk the mayonnaise, yoghurt, apple juice, lemon juice, salt and pepper together in a bowl.

Lightly toast the walnuts in a hot, dry pan for a couple of minutes. Remove any strings from the celery, then finely slice. Quarter and core the apples, then dice finely. Add to the dressing with the celery, walnuts and dill, and toss well.

Finely slice the chicken, add to the salad and toss lightly. Arrange the lettuce leaves on eight dinner plates or one large buffet plate, and spoon the salad on top.

SERVES 8

4 chicken breasts

1 bay leaf

$1/2$ onion

2 tbsp walnuts, roughly chopped

4 celery sticks

2 red or green skinned apples

2 tbsp finely chopped fresh dill

crisp lettuce leaves to serve

Dressing:

1 tbsp quality mayonnaise

1 tbsp natural yoghurt

2 tbsp apple juice

1 tsp lemon juice

sea salt

freshly ground black pepper

Chicken Caesar

It's the most popular thing on the café menu, but we can do it better at home. Note this dressing contains raw egg yolk.

To make the dressing, whiz the egg yolk, garlic, anchovy fillets, mustard, wine vinegar, white wine, salt and pepper in a blender until smooth. With the motor running, gradually add the olive oil.

Heat the grill. Brush the chicken with olive oil and grill gently for 15 minutes, turning once, or until cooked through. Season the chicken with salt and pepper and slice thickly. Grill or fry the bacon until crisp, then crumble into shards.

Grill or toast the bread, then brush with a little olive oil and cut into cubes to make croûtons. Remove the outer lettuce leaves.

Combine the inner lettuce leaves with the croûtons, chicken and half the dressing in a large bowl. Toss gently, then arrange on serving plates. Scatter with the bacon and parmesan, and drizzle with the remaining dressing.

SERVES 4

3 chicken breast fillets

1–2 tbsp extra virgin olive oil

4 rashers rindless bacon

2 thick slices sourdough bread

4 Little Gem lettuces, or 2 Cos

1 tbsp freshly grated parmesan

Dressing:

1 egg yolk

2 garlic cloves, peeled

2 anchovy fillets

1 tsp Dijon mustard

2 tbsp white wine vinegar

1 tbsp white wine

sea salt

freshly ground black pepper

125 ml light olive oil

Asian duck salad

Buy half a Chinese roast duck in Chinatown or use leftover roast duck, and turn it into a light, fresh, crunchy salad with a delicate, sweet dressing. Also good with barbecued chicken.

Slice or shred the duck meat, discarding the bones. Cut the carrots into short lengths, then into matchsticks. Slice the mangetout, sweet pepper and spring onions lengthwise into matchsticks.

Put the carrots, pepper and bean sprouts in a bowl, pour a jug of boiling water over them, then drain and refresh under cold running water. Drain again.

To make the dressing, whisk the mirin, rice vinegar, fish sauce, sugar, salt, pepper and olive oil together in a bowl.

Add the vegetables and duck to the dressing and toss gently. Pile onto plates and serve, with or without steamed rice.

SERVES 4

½ Chinese roast duck, or
leftover roast duck
2 carrots, peeled
200 g mangetout (snow peas)
1 sweet red or yellow pepper,
cored and seeded
2 spring onions, trimmed
200 g bean sprouts

Dressing:
1 tbsp mirin (Japanese
sweet rice wine)
2 tbsp Japanese rice vinegar
1 tbsp fish sauce
1 tsp sugar
sea salt
freshly ground black pepper
3 tbsp olive oil

Torn mozzarella and peppers

I fell in love with this torn salad at Geoff Lindsay's opalescent Pearl restaurant in Melbourne, Australia. It looks like a bottomless pizza, and should be served with crusty bread or warmed flat bread. Fresh buffalo milk mozzarella is heavenly. If you can't find it, you could use good feta or fresh ricotta.

Holding the peppers upright, cut the 'sides' away from the core and seeds, then cut each piece into 1cm squares.

Combine the peppers with the olive oil, sea salt and pepper in a saucepan and stew gently over a low heat for 10 to 15 minutes, without allowing them to 'fry' or brown. Remove from the heat and leave to cool until barely warm.

To serve, set out four dinner plates or one very large platter. Using a slotted spoon, arrange the peppers over the plate, saving the oil. Tear the parsley leaves into shreds with your fingers and scatter over the top.

Drain the mozzarella and pat dry. Tear the soft, fresh cheese into small bits with your fingers, discarding any thick skin, and dot around the plate at random. Drizzle with the reserved oil to serve.

SERVES 4

2 sweet red peppers

2 sweet yellow peppers

2 tbsp extra virgin olive oil

sea salt

freshly ground black pepper

2 tbsp flat-leaf parsley

2 fresh mozzarella bocconcini

(balls), each about 125g

Mallorcan tumbet

I came across these layered baked vegetables in Mallorca, where they are cooked in a terracotta 'cassola'. I'm all for using canned tomatoes to make a sauce, especially in winter.

To make the sauce, combine the tomatoes, oregano, garlic and olive oil with sea salt and pepper in a saucepan, and simmer, covered, for 20 minutes. Heat the oven to 180°C/Gas 4.

Peel and finely slice the potatoes. Finely slice the aubergines. Cut the peppers into long thin fingers, discarding core and seeds. Heat 2 tbsp olive oil in a fry pan and gently fry the potato slices in batches, until golden on both sides. Layer in a 1 litre baking dish and season.

Add the remaining olive oil to the pan and fry the aubergine until well browned. Arrange over the potatoes and season. Fry the red peppers, then layer on top of the aubergines.

Spoon the tomato sauce over the top of the vegetables and bake for 20 minutes until bubbling hot. Serve warm or at room temperature, as a starter or side dish, or as a main course for two.

SERVES 4

400g all-purpose potatoes

400g aubergines (eggplant)

2 sweet red peppers

3 tbsp olive oil

sea salt

freshly ground black pepper

Sauce:

400g canned tomatoes, chopped

3 oregano sprigs, or 1 tsp dried oregano

3 garlic cloves, finely sliced

2 tbsp olive oil

tomatoes

buy the perfect tomato

Buy tomatoes that are good enough to eat in your hands: taut-skinned, green-stemmed, perfumed, ripened on the vine before picking, and brought to the market with stalks intact, which helps them last longer.

how to peel and seed

Cut out the core, and cut a small cross in the base. Drop the tomatoes into a pot of simmering water for 20 seconds, then remove, run under cold water, and slip off the skins. Cut in half, squeeze out and discard the seeds and the juice.

instant tomato sauce

Sizzle a punnet of whole cherry tomatoes with a spoonful of olive oil in a hot non-stick fry pan until the skins burst, then tip the lot over green beans or asparagus, grilled fish, or pan-fried chicken breast – instant sauce.

simple tomato vinaigrette

Peel, seed and dice 2 tomatoes and stir gently through 4 tbsp extra virgin olive oil and 1 tbsp red wine vinegar, sea salt and pepper. Spoon over grilled sea bass or pan-fried salmon.

soft and juicy semi-dried tomatoes

Cut 1kg plum tomatoes lengthwise into three. Arrange on a rack over a tray, sprinkle with sea salt and thyme, and bake at 60°C overnight until semi-dried. Cool, layer in a sterilised jar, top with olive oil, seal and keep refrigerated.

intensify the flavour

Baking reduces water content, and concentrates flavour and acidity. Just cut tomatoes in half, drizzle with olive oil, scatter with sea salt and pepper and bake at 180°C/Gas 4 for 30 to 40 minutes or until they smell interesting.

hot and cold pasta sauce

Peel, seed and roughly chop 4 ripe red tomatoes and douse in extra virgin olive oil with a few smashed garlic cloves and a handful of basil leaves. Leave for a few hours to intensify, then toss the lot through hot linguine.

fast tomato tart

Roll out puff pastry, cut into saucer shapes, brush with egg, prick and bake at 220°C/Gas 7 for 5 minutes. Cover each tart with halved cherry tomatoes tossed in olive oil, basil, sea salt and pepper and bake for 15 minutes until golden.

the 10 minute trick

Add a handful of cherry tomatoes to the last 10 minutes of cooking just about anything – parmesan risotto, Spanish rice, roast leg of lamb – they will turn ruby red, soft and juicy.

easy tomato jam

Seed and chop 1 kg tomatoes. Gently simmer for 1 hour with 3 tbsp brown sugar, 1 tbsp mustard seeds, 2 tbsp red wine vinegar and 3 tbsp olive oil until thick and jammy. Season and cool, then store in airtight jars in the fridge.

Smash them, sizzle them, slice them, or eat them out of your hand.

Tomatoes add instant flavour, acidity, juicy bits,

and film star colour.

Caponata

This is essentially a sweet and sour vegetable stew that began in the caupona, a type of osteria or tavern in southern Italy, which served cooked vegetables. Local sailors bought the vegetables while in port, then ate them flavoured with vinegar and sugar when at sea. Serve with lightly warmed pitta bread or flat bread.

Cut the aubergine into thick slices, then cut each slice into roughly 1cm cubes. Heat 2 tbsp olive oil in a fry pan and fry the aubergine briskly, tossing well, until golden and half cooked. Remove with a slotted spoon and set aside.

Add the remaining olive oil to the fry pan. When hot, add the onion and cook for 5 minutes until soft.

In the meantime, cut the tomatoes in half and squeeze out the seeds. Roughly chop the tomato flesh and add to the pan with the aubergine, celery, bay leaf, olives, salt and pepper. Cook for another 10 minutes.

Dissolve the sugar in the wine vinegar and add to the pan along with the capers. Cook for another 10 minutes until the aubergine is soft and there is no longer a sharp taste of vinegar.

Lightly toast the pine nuts in a hot, dry pan. Lightly warm the bread in a moderate oven or in a hot, dry pan for 2 minutes. Scatter the pine nuts over the vegetables, drizzle with olive oil and serve at room temperature, with a pile of warm bread.

SERVES 4 TO 6
2 medium aubergines (eggplant)
3 tbsp olive oil
1 onion, finely chopped
4 medium tomatoes
2 celery sticks, finely sliced
1 bay leaf
3 tbsp green olives, stoned
sea salt
freshly ground black pepper
1 tbsp sugar
2 tbsp red wine vinegar
1 tbsp capers, rinsed
2 tbsp pine nuts

To serve:
6-8 flat or pitta breads
extra virgin olive oil

Yellow pepper salad

Put these warm, sunny flavours with sliced prosciutto and fresh crusty bread for a lazy lunch, or with barbecued fish, chicken or lamb at any time.

Heat the oven to 200°C/Gas 6. Place the peppers in a baking tin and coat with a little of the olive oil. Bake for 20 minutes, turning once or twice, until lightly scorched. Alternatively you can grill the oiled peppers on a cast-iron grill pan, or under the grill.

Remove peppers from the heat and place in a bowl. Cover and leave for 10 minutes, then peel away the skin, and remove the core and seeds. Cut the flesh lengthwise into thick strips.

Arrange the pepper strips on a serving plate. Combine the olives, remaining olive oil, sea salt and pepper, and drizzle over the top. Scatter with basil leaves or sprigs of thyme.

SERVES 4

2 yellow and 2 orange peppers
   (or 4 yellow ones)
2 tbsp extra virgin olive oil
2 tbsp small black olives
sea salt
freshly ground black pepper
few basil leaves, or thyme
   sprigs

Grilled courgette salad

Slice 6 courgettes (zucchini) lengthwise, brush with olive oil and grill. Whisk 2 tbsp each lemon juice, extra virgin olive oil and chopped dill. Season and pour over the courgettes. Serve topped with grilled lemon.

beets and greens

Green veg frittata

A frittata is an Italian-style omelette that makes a simple lunch or supper. Use Swiss chard (silverbeet), ruby or rainbow chard, cavolo nero (black cabbage) or even green vegetables such as leeks, asparagus, peas and fine green beans.

Cut the stems from the Swiss chard and roughly chop. Cook in a large pot of simmering salted water for 10 minutes. Wash the leaves well, roughly chop, and add to the pot. Cook for 3 or 4 minutes until wilted. Drain well and cool, then squeeze out any excess water.

Beat the eggs, yolks, cream, cheese, salt, pepper and nutmeg in a bowl. Heat the butter and oil in a non-stick fry pan, then pour in the eggs. Scatter in the greens, jiggling them so they settle into the egg.

Cook over a moderate heat until the eggs have set on the bottom and are lightly golden. Heat the grill, protect the fry pan handle with foil and grill the frittata for a few minutes until lightly golden and just set in the middle. If it's still runny, cover the pan and place over a moderate heat for a minute or two. Cut into big wedges and serve.

SERVES 4 TO 6

1 kg Swiss chard (silverbeet)

6 free-range eggs, plus
    2 extra egg yolks

100 ml single cream

80 g freshly grated parmesan
    or gruyère

sea salt

freshly ground black pepper

1/2 tsp freshly grated nutmeg

1 tsp butter

2 tsp olive oil

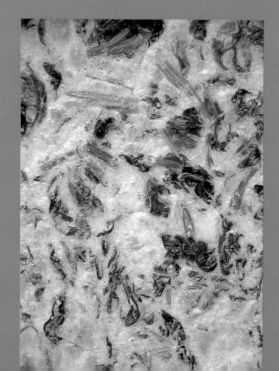

Beets and greens

Buying baby beetroot without its ruby red stems and small bright green leaves is like buying asparagus without the tips. If the tops have already been guillotined, serve the beets on wilted spinach leaves or Swiss chard (silverbeet).

Cut the baby beetroot from their stems and cook unpeeled in simmering salted water for around 45 minutes until tender. Drain and cool, then rub off the skin with your fingers. Rinse well, toss the beets in 1 tbsp of the extra virgin olive oil and set aside.

Wash the leafy stems, and discard the thickest parts of the stems. Roughly chop the leaves and stems, keeping them separate.

Cook the stems in boiling salted water for 2 minutes, then add the leaves and cover. Simmer for 3 minutes until the leaves have wilted and the stems are tender. Drain well, and toss with the remaining extra virgin olive oil, lemon juice, sea salt and pepper.

Arrange on a large platter and tumble the baby beets on top. Serve warm or at room temperature with lemon wedges, as a side dish. Or serve as part of a meal of shared plates, perhaps with marinated feta, grilled lamb, and a tomato and cucumber salad.

SERVES 4

12 baby beetroot, with leaves

$\frac{1}{2}$ tsp salt

3 tbsp extra virgin olive oil

1 tbsp lemon juice

sea salt

freshly ground black pepper

1 lemon, quartered

parsley and lemon salad

Sesame mangetout

Mangetout (snow peas) are too boring for words when cooked whole. But shred them finely and toss raw in a sweet Asian vinaigrette, and they taste wild. Serve as a salad or side dish, or use as a base for seafood, duck or barbecued quail.

Wash and dry the mangetout, then finely slice lengthwise into matchsticks, using the tip of a sharp knife. This will take some time, but keep going and don't curse me too much. The effect it has on the flavour and texture is too great to give up now.

For the dressing, mix the sugar, soy sauce, wine vinegar, rice wine and sesame oil together. Lightly toss the shredded mangetout in the dressing, draining off any excess.

Arrange the dressed mangetout on a serving plate and sprinkle with the sesame seeds to serve.

SERVES 4
250g mangetout (snow peas)
2 tsp sesame seeds

Dressing:
1 tsp sugar
1 tbsp soy sauce
1 tbsp rice wine vinegar, or
    white wine vinegar
1 tbsp Chinese rice wine, or
    dry sherry
2 tsp sesame oil

Parsley and lemon salad

The freshest, brightest, herbiest, tangiest salad around, traditionally eaten wrapped in fresh, unsprayed, vine leaves. It's never as good as when you first make it, so eat soon after.

Rinse the burghul, then soak in cold water to cover for 1 hour, or until swollen.

Chop the spring onions. Peel the cucumber, halve, scoop out the seeds and finely chop the flesh. Cut the tomatoes in half, squeeze out and discard the seeds and juice, and dice the flesh.

Pick off the herb leaves, wash and dry well, then roughly chop. Drain the burghul and squeeze dry. Toss with the herbs, spring onions, cucumber and tomato.

Mix the olive oil with the lemon juice, cumin, cayenne and sea salt. Pour the dressing over the salad, toss well and serve.

SERVES 4

150g fine burghul
(bulgur wheat)
2 spring onions
1 small cucumber
2 tomatoes
2 bunches of parsley
1 bunch of mint

Dressing:
2 tbsp extra virgin olive oil
2 tbsp lemon juice
$\frac{1}{2}$ tsp ground cumin
$\frac{1}{2}$ tsp cayenne pepper
1 tsp sea salt

Cabbage with cumin

How to turn a cabbage hater into a cabbage lover: buy the smallest, brightest, crispest and heaviest cabbage you can find, preferably the crinkly-leafed Savoy, cook it quickly and serve in a vinaigrette with cumin seeds.

Bring a large pan of water to the boil. Trim the base of the cabbage, but don't cut out the entire core as this will hold the wedges together. Cut the cabbage in half from top to bottom and then cut each half into three equal wedges. Discard the outer leaves that aren't up to scratch.

Add the salt to the boiling water and cook the cabbage wedges for 5 to 10 minutes or until they start to soften. Drain them well, upside down in a colander.

Whisk the olive oil, wine vinegar, sugar, sea salt and pepper together in a bowl to make a vinaigrette. Arrange the cabbages on a serving platter and spoon over the vinaigrette. Scatter with cumin or caraway seeds and serve.

SERVES 4 TO 6

1 small, tight Savoy cabbage, around 1 kg

½ tsp salt

1 tbsp olive oil

1 tbsp white wine vinegar

1 tsp caster sugar

sea salt

freshly ground black pepper

2 tsp cumin or caraway seeds

Pumpkin with raclette

Naturally sweet vegetables, such as pumpkin and butternut squash, are fantastic teamed with cheese. Raclette, fontina, and taleggio are all good melting cheeses, or use fresh mozzarella. Serve with a simple roast or a leafy green vegetable.

Heat the oven to 200°C/Gas 6. Cut the pumpkin or squash roughly into 2.5cm cubes, cutting off any skin and discarding the seeds.

Steam the pumpkin cubes over fast boiling water for 20 minutes until tender, then drain and pile into a heatproof bowl or gratin dish. (If you don't have a steamer, put the cubes in a baking tray, add a dash of water, cover with foil and bake for 30 minutes or until tender.)

Cut the cheese into thin slices. Bake the pumpkin for 10 minutes or so, to help dry out the rather watery flesh, then top with the slices of cheese and bake for another minute or two until melted. Scatter with sea salt, pepper, oregano, sage and thyme, and serve.

SERVES 4

1 kg pumpkin or butternut squash

150 g raclette or other melting cheese

sea salt

freshly ground black pepper

few oregano sprigs

1 tbsp sage leaves

few thyme sprigs

Peas and bacon

Peas should be revered as they were in the seventeenth century, when the sophisticated Madame de Maintenon from the French court of Louis XIV wrote of the royal courtiers' obsession with peas as 'both a fashion and a madness'.

Cook the peas in simmering salted water until just tender. Drain, refresh with cold water, drain well and set aside. (You can do this ahead of time.)

SERVES 4

600g podded fresh or
frozen peas

salt

6 shallots, or 1 small red onion

100g thick rindless bacon
rashers

2 tbsp butter

100ml chicken stock or dry
white wine

1 tsp caster sugar

sea salt

freshly ground black pepper

Peel and slice the shallots, and finely chop the bacon. Heat half the butter in a pan and gently cook the shallots and bacon for 5 minutes. Add the stock or wine and bring to the boil, then reduce to a simmer.

Add the peas, sugar, sea salt, plenty of black pepper and the remaining butter. Gently heat through and simmer until the liquid is reduced to a couple of tablespoonfuls, then serve.

paper bag veggies

Paper bag veggies

A splendid vegetarian dinner is in the bag with these baked paper 'purses' of steamy spiced vegetables, served with a bowl of garlicky herbed crème fraîche. Make sure you have enough greaseproof or baking paper to make the bags.

Heat the oven to 200°C/Gas 6. Trim the leeks and cut into 1 cm slices. Peel the potatoes, sweet potato and parsnips, and cut into chunky bite-sized pieces. Cut the courgettes and red pepper into similar pieces, discarding the pepper core and seeds.

In a large bowl, mix the olive oil with the saffron, thyme, rosemary, sea salt and pepper. Add the vegetables and toss well.

Cut four rounds of greaseproof paper, 36 cm in diameter. Divide the vegetables between them, scatter with fennel seeds and bring the paper up evenly around each pile of vegetables, pursing it together at the top and tying securely with string.

Place the bags on a baking sheet and bake for 30 to 40 minutes or until an inserted skewer meets with no resistance. Meanwhile, beat the garlic and parsley into the crème fraîche and set aside.

To serve, snip the paper parcels open below the string, and serve in or out of the paper, with the herbed crème fraîche.

SERVES 4

2 leeks

4 smallish potatoes

1 medium sweet potato

2 medium parsnips

2 medium courgettes

1 sweet red pepper

4 tbsp extra virgin olive oil

½ tsp powdered saffron

4 thyme sprigs

4 rosemary sprigs

sea salt

freshly ground black pepper

1 tbsp fennel seeds

To serve:

2 garlic cloves, crushed

2 tbsp finely chopped parsley

200 g crème fraîche

Black olive roast veg

I always keep a jar of pesto and a jar of olive tapenade in the fridge door next to the Campari and soda. They're great instant flavour hits if you don't want to do much more than grill some sourdough bread or cook some pasta for dinner.

Heat the oven to 200°C/Gas 6. Cut the pumpkin into thinnish wedges, trim off the skin, and discard any seeds. Peel the potatoes and cut in half. Wash the carrots, trim the tops neatly, and peel. Peel the parsnips and cut lengthwise into quarters.

Combine the tapenade with the olive oil and pepper in a big bowl. Add the vegetables, rosemary and garlic cloves and toss until well coated. Tip into a baking tray and bake for 45 minutes to 1 hour, until the vegetables are tender and nicely browned.

Pile the roast vegetables onto warm plates and tuck in a few fresh rosemary sprigs. Top with a spoonful of olive tapenade, thinned with a little olive oil.

SERVES 4

500g pumpkin
500g smallish potatoes
2 bunches baby carrots
4 parsnips
2 tbsp black olive tapenade
2 tbsp extra virgin olive oil
1/2 tsp freshly ground black pepper
4 rosemary sprigs
4 garlic cloves (unpeeled)

To serve:
rosemary sprigs
extra black olive tapenade
a little extra virgin olive oil

Vegetable curry

For me, an Indian vegetable curry should be warmly spiced, rather than chilli-hot, with meltingly soft vegetables, and a sauce that calls for a huge mound of rice. Done.

Finely slice the onion. Peel and roughly chop the potatoes. Peel and quarter the carrot and parsnips lengthwise. Cut the aubergine, courgette and red pepper into chunks, discarding the pepper core and seeds.

Heat the oil in a heavy-based frying pan and add the mustard seeds and fenugreek. When the seeds start to pop, add the cumin, turmeric, ginger and paprika, stirring. Add the onion and cook for 5 minutes until softened.

Add the potatoes and fry lightly, then add the carrot, parsnips, aubergine, courgette and red pepper, stirring. Add the water, tomato purée, salt, sugar, curry leaves and cinnamon stick, and bring to the boil.

Simmer, uncovered, for 30 to 40 minutes or until the vegetables are soft and the liquid is reduced to a sauce, stirring occasionally. Serve with plenty of rice.

SERVES 4

1 onion, peeled

500g all-purpose potatoes

1 carrot, peeled

2 parsnips, peeled

1 aubergine (eggplant)

1 courgette (zucchini)

1 sweet red pepper

2 tbsp vegetable oil

2 tsp mustard seeds

$\frac{1}{2}$ tsp fenugreek seeds

1 tsp ground cumin

1 tsp ground turmeric

1 tsp ground ginger

$\frac{1}{2}$ tsp paprika

1 litre water or stock

1 tbsp tomato purée (paste)

1 tsp salt

1 tsp soft brown sugar

few curry leaves

1 cinnamon stick

toss with dill, parsley or chives

Warm potatoes and capers

Cold potatoes are an abomination, but something quite special happens when warm potatoes hit a generous, mustardy dressing. Eat warm, obviously.

Cook the potatoes in simmering, salted water until tender but still firm, about 20 minutes. Finely chop the spring onions.

In the meantime, make the dressing. Combine the olive oil, wine vinegar, mustard, sea salt and pepper in a large bowl and whisk well until thickened. Add the capers, spring onions and chopped herbs, and toss lightly.

Drain the potatoes and slice them thickly, as soon as you can handle them. Toss them carefully in the dressing, making sure the slices don't stick together. Arrange on warmed plates, drizzle with any extra dressing and serve.

SERVES 4

6 medium waxy potatoes, peeled
3 spring onions
1 tbsp small capers, rinsed
2 tbsp chopped dill, parsley or chives

Dressing:
3 tbsp extra virgin olive oil
2 tbsp red wine vinegar
1 tsp Dijon mustard
sea salt
freshly ground black pepper

Chorizo and sweet potato

Cut 2 cooked sweet potatoes and
4 chorizo sausages thickly on the
diagonal, brush with oil and grill
until sizzling. Whisk 1 tbsp
lemon juice and 2 tbsp olive
oil with 1 tbsp chopped
parsley, then toss with
200 g rocket leaves. Pile
the sizzling sweet potatoes
and sausages on top.

potatoes

Potato and borlotti mash Cook 1 kg potatoes with 2 peeled garlic cloves until tender, adding 400g drained, canned borlotti beans for the last minute. Drain and return to the pan. Add 2 tbsp extra virgin olive oil, 1 tbsp chopped parsley, sea salt and pepper. Mash, keeping it chunky.

Greek red potatoes Par-boil 1 kg peeled, quartered waxy potatoes for 10 minutes; drain. Toss with 2 tbsp tomato purée, 2 tbsp extra virgin olive oil, 2 tbsp water, salt and pepper. Bake on a foil-lined tray at 200°C/Gas 6 for 20 minutes until tender. Serve with roast lamb or grilled fish.

Floury or waxy? Use floury potatoes such as King Edward, Maris Piper, pink-skinned Desirée and Romano for mashing, roasting and frying. Choose waxy potatoes – Charlotte, La Ratte, Jersey Royal, Kipfler, Belle de Fontenay and Pink Fir Apple – for simple boiled potatoes and salads.

Warm saffron potato salad Whisk 2 tbsp extra virgin olive oil with 1 tbsp mayonnaise, 1 tbsp lemon juice, 1 tsp tomato purée, 1 tsp Dijon mustard, $^{1}/_{2}$ tsp powdered saffron, $^{1}/_{2}$ tsp paprika, sea salt and pepper. Thickly slice 1 kg boiled potatoes. Toss in the dressing while still warm.

Potato, tuna and olive salad Drain and flake 400g canned tuna in oil. Whisk 3 tbsp extra virgin olive oil, 3 tbsp white wine and 2 tbsp lemon juice with salt and pepper. Thickly slice 600g boiled waxy potatoes and toss in the dressing. Add the tuna and 20 black olives. Serve with rocket.

Is it cooked? When you boil potatoes, spear one with a thin bamboo skewer so the stick pokes up out of the water. To check if the potatoes are cooked, pick up the bamboo stick. If the potato clings to it, it's not yet cooked. If it slips off, it's perfect. Brilliant!

Goose fat potatoes Peel 3 medium waxy potatoes and cut into 2cm dice. Fry gently in 100g goose or duck fat with 2 garlic cloves for 20 minutes, tossing occasionally, then turn up the heat and cook until crisp and brown. Drain, toss with sea salt and pepper, and serve.

Belgian stoemp Cook 750g potatoes with 3 finely sliced leeks until tender. Drain and lightly mash with butter, salt, pepper and a little grated nutmeg. Serve with sausages, grilled fish or a thick slice of leg ham.

Herring and potato salad Dress 600g hot boiled potatoes with 2 tbsp olive oil, 2 tbsp white wine, 2 tbsp red wine vinegar and 1 tbsp Dijon mustard. Add a dollop of sour cream, 1 tbsp capers, lots of pepper, and a little finely sliced shallot. Drape 4 marinated herrings on top.

Choucroûte for cheats Cook 1kg small peeled potatoes until tender. Heat 300g prepared sauerkraut in a pan with 1 tsp caraway seeds and 100ml white wine. Simmer 4 frankfurters and 4 weisswurst for 5 minutes, drain and serve on the sauerkraut and potatoes, with Dijon mustard.

Smoked salmon potato Prick 4 large baking potatoes, coat lightly in olive oil and roll in a little sea salt and cracked black pepper. Bake at 200°C/Gas 6 for 1$^1/_2$ hours until soft. Cut open, top with crème fraîche, smoked salmon, horseradish sauce and chives.

Six more baked potato toppings Bake 4 large potatoes (as above), and top with: poached egg and crisped bacon; caramelised onions; pan-fried mushrooms and chives; pan-fried chicken livers; wilted rocket and gorgonzola; or roasted red peppers tossed with capers and anchovies.

goose fat potatoes

dinners

Chinese roast pork

This isn't as scary as you think it's going to be. A good piece of belly pork is the easiest roast in the world, giving you tender meat topped with lots of crisp crackling. Serve sliced with steamed rice and Chinese greens, or cut into fingers to dip into hoisin sauce as a starter.

Wash and dry the belly pork, and score the skin at 1cm intervals (for easy slicing later). Combine the salt and five spice powder and rub it all over the skin and meat. Set aside in the fridge for at least 2 hours.

Heat the oven to 230°C/Gas 8. Line a roasting tray with foil and place the pork on a rack set above the foil. Bake for 20 minutes.

SERVES 4

1 kg piece fresh belly pork

1 tbsp salt

3 tsp Chinese five spice powder

4 tbsp hoisin sauce

Lower the oven setting to 200°C/Gas 6 and bake for a further 45 minutes or until the skin crackles and crisps. If it doesn't totally crisp, finish the pork under the grill, being careful not to let it blister too much.

Remove the pork from the oven, and cut out any bones from the base. Cut the pork into thick slices, and then into thick fingers if you like. Serve warm, with hoisin sauce for dipping.

Pork chop with capers

A caper is a frisky leap or a dance. It's also the unopened flower bud of *Capparis spinosa*, a straggly, unkempt Mediterranean shrub. When cured, each little bud has the same sort of frisky effect in the mouth, especially in this lemony parsley dressing. Serve with a rocket salad and potatoes or a pumpkin mash.

To cook the pork chops, heat the olive oil in a non-stick frying pan. Lightly dust the chops in the flour, seasoned with salt, pepper and paprika; shake off any excess. Cook on one side over a moderate heat for around 8 minutes. Turn and cook on the other side for 5 minutes or until tender.

To make the dressing, pick the leaves from the parsley stems. Halve the tomato, squeeze out the seeds and juice, and finely chop the flesh. Mix the chopped tomato with the capers, parsley leaves, olive oil and lemon juice. Season with sea salt and pepper, and stir well.

Season the pork chops and place on warmed serving plates. Use a slotted spoon to spoon the dressing on and around each pork chop. Top with caper berries.

SERVES 4
4 large pork rib chops
2 tbsp olive oil
2 tbsp plain flour
$\frac{1}{2}$ tsp sea salt
$\frac{1}{2}$ tsp freshly ground black pepper
$\frac{1}{2}$ tsp smoked paprika or cayenne pepper
8 caper berries

Dressing:
good handful of flat-leaf parsley
1 ripe red tomato
1 tbsp capers, rinsed
3 tbsp extra virgin olive oil
1 tbsp lemon juice

Pork with apple and sage

Top a seared pork chop with a juicy baked apple, and you have an instant fresh apple sauce on the plate.

Heat the oven to 180°C/Gas 4. Finely chop the onion. Mash 1 tbsp butter with the chopped onion, sugar and 4 sage leaves. Core the apples from the bottom, leaving the stalk intact at the top. Fill each hollow with the stuffing.

Stand the apples in a small baking tin, add the white wine, then pour in enough boiling water to come halfway up the side of the apples. Bake for 45 minutes, or until soft and squishy.

Heat the olive oil and remaining 1 tbsp butter in a heavy-based fry pan with 4 sage leaves. Add the pork chops and cook over moderate heat for around 8 to 10 minutes. Season well with sea salt and pepper. Turn the chops and cook for another 5 minutes or until tender.

Place the pork chops on warmed plates, top with the baked apples and tuck in the remaining sage leaves. Serve with mash.

SERVES 4

½ onion, peeled

2 tbsp butter

1 tbsp sugar

12 sage leaves

4 crisp, tart eating apples
    (eg Granny Smith)

250 ml dry white wine

1 tbsp olive oil

4 thick pork loin chops

sea salt

freshly ground black pepper

instant apple sauce

Ham and mushroom pie

A nice big pie all to myself is my idea of comfort food, especially when frozen puff pastry makes it so simple.

Heat the oven to 200°C/Gas 6. Strip the thyme leaves from their stems. Heat the olive oil in a fry pan and gently cook the onion, garlic and thyme for 5 minutes. Slice the mushrooms, add to the pan and cook for 10 minutes until soft.

Shred the cooked ham or chicken, discarding any bones or skin. Off the heat, add to the mushroom mixture with the cooked peas. Season well with salt and pepper.

To make the sauce, melt the butter in a small saucepan, add the flour and cook, stirring, over a gentle heat for 3 minutes. Add a few spoonfuls of chicken stock and stir well, then add the remaining stock and bring to the boil, stirring constantly as the sauce thickens.

Add the cream, Worcestershire sauce, mustard, nutmeg and cayenne, and simmer gently for a couple of minutes, stirring. Add salt and pepper to taste, then strain the sauce over the filling and toss well.

Divide the filling between four individual pie dishes. Cover the tops with pastry, trimming to fit. Brush with beaten egg and bake for 30 minutes until puffy and golden.

MAKES 4

6 thyme sprigs
1 tbsp olive oil
1 onion, finely chopped
2 garlic cloves, smashed
500g button mushrooms
450g cooked ham or chicken
200g podded fresh or frozen peas, cooked
sea salt
freshly ground black pepper
500g packet ready-rolled frozen puff pastry, thawed
1 free-range egg, beaten

Sauce:
1 tbsp butter
1 tbsp flour
250ml chicken stock
2 tbsp cream
1 tbsp Worcestershire sauce
1 tsp Dijon mustard
$1/2$ tsp ground nutmeg
$1/2$ tsp cayenne pepper

drunken potatoes

Lamb with tomatoes and olives

I grew up with the time-honoured roast lamb every Sunday, followed by variations on a theme of lamb most evenings during the week. You'd think I'd be over it, but instead I love cooking lamb at home, and ordering lamb when eating out. This is typical of the sort of thing I do at home when I'm pushed for time.

Place the lamb steaks between two sheets of cling film or greaseproof paper and bash them flat with a meat mallet or rolling pin. Place in a shallow dish and toss in the olive oil, garlic and rosemary sprigs.

Heat a non-stick fry pan. When it is very hot, add the lamb (saving the marinade) and sear very quickly for a minute or two on each side, turning once. Remove the lamb to a plate while still pink inside, season with sea salt and pepper, and let it rest for a minute or two while you do the tomatoes.

Tip the reserved marinade into the pan, and add the cherry tomatoes and olives. Warm through until the tomatoes start to soften and burst.

Slice the lamb and arrange on warm plates. Tip the tomatoes and olives over the lamb and serve.

SERVES 4

4 lamb steaks, around 180g
   each, or 2 lamb loin fillets
   (cut in two)
2 tbsp extra virgin olive oil
2 garlic cloves, smashed
2 rosemary sprigs
sea salt
freshly ground black pepper
200g cherry tomatoes
100g small black olives
   (eg Niçoise or Ligurian)

Drunken potatoes

This is my favourite new way of roasting potatoes because they absorb the flavour of the white wine they're cooked in, then turn crisp at the edges. For all those who loved the crash hot potatoes that appeared in Simple Food, you owe it to yourself to move on. Serve with grilled or pan-fried meat, poultry or fish, such as lamb with tomatoes (left), salt and pepper steak (page 182), jump-in-the-pan chicken (page 193), or cod in prosciutto (page 204).

Heat the oven to 200°C / Gas 6. Peel the potatoes and finely slice crosswise. Toss the potato slices in a bowl with the olive oil, sea salt and pepper. Lightly oil a baking tray (or deep-rimmed baking sheet) and scatter the potatoes loosely over the base. Pour over the white wine and scatter with the thyme.

Bake for 30 minutes, during which time the wine will boil and bubble away, and the potatoes will crisp to a beautiful golden crunch. Keep an eye on them during the last few minutes after the wine has evaporated, as they can over-crisp. The slices in the corners might get scorched, but it's worth the sacrifice.

Use a fish slice to lift the potatoes out of the pan, and serve hot.

SERVES 4

3 large, long potatoes,
around 750g
2 tbsp extra virgin olive oil
sea salt
freshly ground black pepper
250ml dry white wine
1 tbsp thyme sprigs

aubergine and lamb

Aubergine and lamb

Lamb fillets are much more interesting if they are bashed flat and quickly seared, leaving them nice and juicy inside.

Flatten the lamb with a meat mallet. Mix 2 tbsp olive oil with the lemon juice, rosemary and thyme, and use to coat the lamb.

Heat the grill. Slice each aubergine lengthwise into eight 1cm thin, flat slices. Brush with olive oil, season with salt and pepper, and grill on both sides until scorched and tender.

Meanwhile, remove spinach stalks and wash the leaves well. Stuff the wet leaves into a saucepan and cook gently, covered, without any extra water, for a few minutes until wilted. Drain and keep warm.

Heat the grill, or a cast-iron grill pan or heavy-based fry pan, until hot. Cook the lamb for 2 minutes on either side (1 minute for small fillets). Season well, and rest on a warm plate.

Gently squeeze the spinach dry, and toss with a little olive oil, salt and pepper. Place a grilled aubergine slice on each warmed plate. Top with spinach, more aubergine, then lamb, and finally spinach. Spoon the pesto on top and serve.

SERVES 4

4 lamb fillets or boneless leg
   steaks, around 180g each
   (or eight 100g fillets)
3–4 tbsp extra virgin olive oil
1 tbsp lemon juice
3 rosemary sprigs
10 thyme sprigs
2 large aubergines (eggplant)
sea salt
freshly ground black pepper
1kg spinach (not baby)
2 tbsp pesto

Crash hot potatoes

This is one of those crazy little recipes that once tried, is immediately incorporated into your own repertoire. It's what you want when you want a crisp, roast potato, only better. And all you have to do is boil some small potatoes, smash them flat and blast them in a hot oven until they are terminally crisp. Serve with aubergine and lamb (see left), pan-fried fish, grilled sausages, or even on their own, with drinks.

Heat the oven to 250°C/Gas 9. Don't peel the potatoes. Just bung them into a pot of salted water, bring to the boil and simmer for around 15 minutes, until they'll take a skewer without too much resistance. They should be just about cooked, without being soft.

Drain the potatoes and arrange on a lightly oiled baking tray. Use a potato masher to squash each potato flat, until it is twice its original diameter. Brush the tops with olive oil, and scatter with sea salt, black pepper, fennel seeds and thyme sprigs.

Bake the potatoes on the top shelf of the oven for 20 to 25 minutes until crisp and golden. Serve hot.

SERVES 4
16 small, round potatoes
salt
1 tbsp extra virgin olive oil
1 tsp sea salt
freshly ground black pepper
1 tbsp fennel or caraway seeds
small handful of thyme sprigs

Salt and pepper steak

One of the tricks of good simple cooking is to upgrade your salt and pepper. I love soft-flaked Maldon sea salt, and buy fresh-tasting vine-ripened peppercorns from India. Sea salt is added to this pepper-crusted steak after cooking, not before, as it would draw out the juices from the meat. Serve with wilted spinach and potatoes.

Crush the peppercorns, then place in a fine sieve and shake to discard any fine dust. Tip the pepper onto a flat plate and press one side of each steak only into the mixture.

Heat the olive oil in a heavy non-stick frying pan. When hot, add the steaks, pepper-side down, and cook for 3 minutes over a moderate heat, without moving them. Turn once and cook for 2 to 3 minutes, depending on thickness. Transfer the steaks to warm plates.

Add the butter to the pan and melt. Add the brandy (carefully as it might flame), stirring well. Add the cream, mustard and a pinch of salt, stirring briskly as it bubbles. Pour into a warm jug. Scatter extra sea salt on the steaks and serve with the mustard sauce.

SERVES 2

1 tbsp black peppercorns

2 good rump or sirloin steaks, 200g each

1 tbsp olive oil

2 tbsp butter

1 tbsp brandy or Cognac

80ml double cream

2 tsp Dijon mustard

sea salt (eg Maldon)

Beef sukiyaki

This isn't the traditional cook-at-the-table dish, but a quick dinner of beef and cellophane noodles. These thin, dried, white noodles are made from mung bean flour – you will find them in oriental food stores.

Pour boiling water over the noodles to cover them and let stand for 3 minutes. Cut the tofu into cubes. Finely chop the spring onions and white onion. Slice the beef as finely as you can.

In a small pan, combine the water and dashi powder, then add the soy sauce, mirin and sugar and heat gently, stirring. Rinse the soaked noodles in cold water, drain and set aside.

Heat half the oil in a heavy-based fry pan, and cook all the onions until soft. Add the noodles, tofu, spinach and dashi sauce, bring to the boil and simmer for 2 to 3 minutes.

Heat the remaining oil in a second fry pan until hot, and sear the beef slices for a few seconds until just cooked but still pink. Divide the noodle mixture between warmed bowls or plates and top with the seared beef. Serve with rice.

SERVES 4

200g cellophane noodles
200g fresh tofu
4 spring onions
1 white onion, peeled
400g best beef fillet
125ml water
10g instant dashi powder
3 tbsp soy sauce
3 tbsp mirin (Japanese sweet rice wine)
1 tbsp sugar
2 tbsp groundnut or peanut oil
200g spinach leaves, well rinsed

Korean beef in lettuce

Tender beef is marinated in soy, garlic, ginger, spring onions and sesame oil, then flash-fried – so quickly that you need everyone waiting at the table before you begin.

Slice the beef thinly, against the grain. For the marinade, finely slice the spring onions and mix with the other ingredients; stir to dissolve the sugar. Add the beef, turn to coat and marinate for an hour or so.

Wash and dry the lettuce leaves; chill. For the soy chilli sauce, mix the sauces together in a bowl and set aside. Cook the jasmine rice until tender; keep warm.

Heat a heavy fry pan. When hot, sear the beef over high heat for 1 to 2 minutes, leaving it still pink in the middle. Scatter with sesame seeds and serve on warm plates, with hot rice and chilled lettuce.

Spoon a little jasmine rice onto a lettuce leaf, add a slice or two of spicy beef and a little soy chilli sauce, wrap the lettuce leaf around the filling and eat in the hands.

SERVES 4

2 sirloin steaks, 2.5 cm thick
and around 250 g each
8 soft lettuce leaves (eg
round, butter, oak leaf)
200 g jasmine rice
1 tbsp sesame seeds

Marinade:
2 spring onions
2 garlic cloves, crushed
5 cm knob of fresh root
ginger, grated
1 tbsp sesame oil
2 tbsp rice wine or dry sherry
3 tbsp soy sauce
1 tbsp sweet chilli sauce or
chilli bean sauce
$1/2$ tsp ground black pepper
1 tbsp sugar

Soy chilli sauce:
2 tbsp soy sauce
2 tbsp sweet chilli sauce or
chilli bean sauce

Roast pesto chicken

This is a good trick: stuff pesto and breadcrumbs under the skin to protect the chicken breast from drying out, and you also infuse it with warm peppery basil.

Heat the oven to 200°C/Gas 6. Wash the chicken breasts and pat dry. Combine the pesto and breadcrumbs in a small bowl to make a thick paste, adding a little olive oil if it's too dry.

Work your fingers in between the skin and meat to create a space, leaving the skin attached at one end or along one side. Stuff the pesto mixture under the skin to cover the breast, carefully draw the skin back over it, and reshape.

Heat a non-stick fry pan, add 1 tbsp oil and sear the chicken skin for a minute or two until lightly golden, then place the chicken skin-side up on a baking tray and drizzle with remaining olive oil, lemon juice, sea salt and pepper.

Bake for about 20 minutes, depending on size, until cooked through. Rest for 5 minutes before serving, with a rocket or watercress salad.

SERVES 4

4 chicken breasts with skin, around 200g each

2 tbsp pesto

2 tbsp fine dry breadcrumbs

2 tbsp extra virgin olive oil

1 tbsp lemon juice

sea salt

freshly ground black pepper

Chicken tikka

Yes, you can make Punjabi-style chicken tikka without investing in a tandoor oven. For the best flavour, use leg or thigh rather than breast meat.

Cut the meat into cubes, about 5 cm square. Combine the yoghurt, lemon juice, garlic, ginger, spices, salt and vegetable oil in a non-reactive bowl, and mix well. Add the chicken, toss well and leave to marinate for 2 to 3 hours.

Heat the grill. Skewer the chicken pieces loosely on thin bamboo skewers, and place on a lightly oiled grill rack. Grill the chicken under a medium heat for about 5 minutes on each side, until nicely scorched and cooked through. (Alternatively you can place the rack over a baking tray and bake in a preheated oven at 230°C/Gas 8 for 10 to 12 minutes.)

Scatter with coriander or parsley, and serve the chicken tikka with lemon wedges and basmati rice.

SERVES 4
450 g boneless chicken meat
150 g yoghurt
2 tbsp lemon juice
2 garlic cloves, peeled and crushed
1 tbsp finely grated fresh ginger
2 tsp garam masala
$\frac{1}{2}$ tsp ground cumin
1 tsp paprika
$\frac{1}{2}$ tsp cayenne powder
1 tsp salt
2 tbsp vegetable oil
handful of coriander or parsley
lemon wedges, to serve

Jump-in-the-pan chicken

This is an action dish, a simple sauté in the pan that creates its own creamy lemon and caper sauce for chicken. It's a terrific idea when you bring home the usual chicken breast and want to do something really fast. The trick is to keep the pan moving, jiggling it on the heat to make the chicken jump. Serve with rice, noodles or mash, or just a green salad.

Place each chicken breast between two sheets of cling film or greaseproof paper and bash flat with a meat mallet or rolling pin, and I mean as thin as a coin – almost breaking up.

Tear the chicken into little rags with your fingers, and toss lightly in the flour, seasoned with salt and pepper.

Heat the olive oil and butter in a large, heavy-based frying pan. When hot, add the chicken, scattering the pieces so they don't clump together. Instead of stirring, move the pan on the heat and flip the chicken pieces until lightly golden, so they jump in the pan.

Add the garlic, bay leaves, capers, sea salt and pepper. Remove the pan from the heat, add the wine, and return to a high heat. Let the wine bubble away, again jiggling the pan like crazy.

When there is only a little wine left, add the lemon juice and parsley leaves, and jiggle the pan until the sauce comes together and looks creamy. Serve immediately.

SERVES 4

3 skinless chicken breasts, around 150g each

2 tbsp plain flour

sea salt

freshly ground black pepper

2 tbsp olive oil

1 tbsp butter

1 garlic clove, crushed

4 bay leaves

2 tbsp capers, well rinsed

125 ml dry white wine

1 tbsp lemon juice

2 tbsp flat-leaf parsley

Chicken and chickpea stew

A very satisfying chicken stew that takes some of the typical ingredients and flavours of Spain – sherry, paprika, chorizo sausages – and turns them into a lively, spicy winter meal you can have on the table within an hour of walking in the door.

Peel the carrots and potatoes and cut into bite-sized pieces. Dust the chicken lightly with flour, seasoned with salt and pepper. Heat 2 tbsp olive oil in a heavy fry pan and brown the chicken pieces.

Add the garlic, carrots, potatoes, paprika, bay leaves, salt and pepper. Add the sherry and water and bring to the boil, then simmer, covered, for about 20 minutes. Add the chickpeas, and cook for another 10 minutes or until the chicken is tender.

Thickly slice the chorizo and pan-fry in the remaining olive oil until sizzling. Add to the stew, scatter with parsley and serve.

SERVES 4

300g carrots

500g potatoes

8 chicken pieces (eg leg, thigh, breast)

1 tbsp plain flour

sea salt

freshly ground black pepper

3 tbsp olive oil

2 garlic cloves, smashed

1 tsp paprika

2 bay leaves

100ml dry sherry

250ml water

400g canned chickpeas, rinsed

2 chorizo sausages, mild or hot

2 tbsp flat-leaf parsley

fast roast fish

Chinese ginger fish

A quick, easy meal for everyone who loves Cantonese-style steamed fish. The fish is best with the skin left on, as the final hot dressing will cause it to sizzle and crisp, but if you don't like the skin, you can peel it off before steaming.

Peel the ginger and cut into tiny matchsticks. Finely slice the chilli and spring onions. Gently wash the fish, pat dry and arrange on a heatproof platter that will fit into your steamer.

SERVES 4

5cm knob of fresh ginger

1 small red chilli

3 spring onions

4 thick fresh fish fillets, with skin (eg bream, haddock, plaice, cod), around 180g each

3 tbsp soy sauce

1 tbsp sesame oil

2 tbsp Chinese rice wine, or dry sherry

1 tbsp sugar

4 tbsp groundnut or peanut oil

3 tbsp coriander leaves

Mix the soy, sesame oil, rice wine and sugar together, and pour over the fish, skin-side up. Scatter the ginger, chilli and half the spring onions on top and steam for 8 to 10 minutes, until the flesh parts easily when pierced with a knife.

Transfer the fish to warmed dinner plates and strain the juices over the top. Heat the oil in a small pan until it just starts to smoke, then pour it over the fish. Scatter with the remaining spring onions and coriander, and serve with jasmine rice.

Fast roast fish

A fabulous way with fish that gives you moist, juicy, good looking fillets in 10 minutes flat. Buy the fattest, freshest fish fillets you can find.

Place a baking tray in the oven and heat the oven to 250°C/Gas 9. The tray may buckle slightly in the heat, but carry on regardless.

In the meantime, gently wash the fish and pat dry. Combine the olive oil, parsley, sea salt and pepper in a bowl, and coat each fish fillet well in the mixture. Cut the lemon into 4 thick slices.

When very hot, remove the tray from the oven and place the fish on its hot surface. Add the lemon slices, return to the top shelf of the oven and bake for 10 minutes. If you could only find thin fillets, test after 5 or 6 minutes.

Gently lift each fish fillet onto a warm dinner plate. Top with a warm slice of lemon, letting its juices run over the fish, and serve.

SERVES 4
4 thick white fish fillets (eg turbot, cod, haddock, hake), around 200g each
2 tbsp extra virgin olive oil
1 tbsp finely chopped parsley
sea salt
freshly ground pepper
1 lemon

Caramel salmon and lime

An unbeatable combination of Thai tastes – chilli, coriander, mint, sugar, lime juice and fish sauce – is just the thing for delicate, rich, flesh-pink salmon.

To make the sauce, dissolve the sugar in the water in a small pan and bring to the boil, stirring. Add the chilli, ginger and garlic, and let it bubble away to reduce (but not boil over) for 4 to 5 minutes until quite syrupy. Remove from the heat, and add the fish sauce and lime juice.

SERVES 4

4 thick salmon fillets, around 180g each

200g bean sprouts

2 tbsp vegetable oil

50g mint leaves

25g coriander leaves

1 spring onion, finely sliced

2 tbsp salted peanuts, crushed

1 lime, quartered

Sauce:

100g soft brown sugar

125ml water

1 red chilli, finely sliced

3cm knob of fresh ginger, finely sliced

2 garlic cloves, peeled and smashed

4 tbsp Thai fish sauce

4 tbsp lime juice

Cut the salmon into bite-sized pieces, about 3cm square, and coat lightly in the caramel sauce.

Pour a jug of boiling water over the bean sprouts, then drain and set aside.

Heat the oil in a non-stick fry pan, and fry the salmon quickly until caramelised, keeping the inside pink.

Combine the salmon, mint, coriander, spring onion and bean sprouts in a bowl, and toss well. Arrange on warmed dinner plates, spoon the warm sauce over the top, and scatter with peanuts. Serve with lime quarters and plenty of rice.

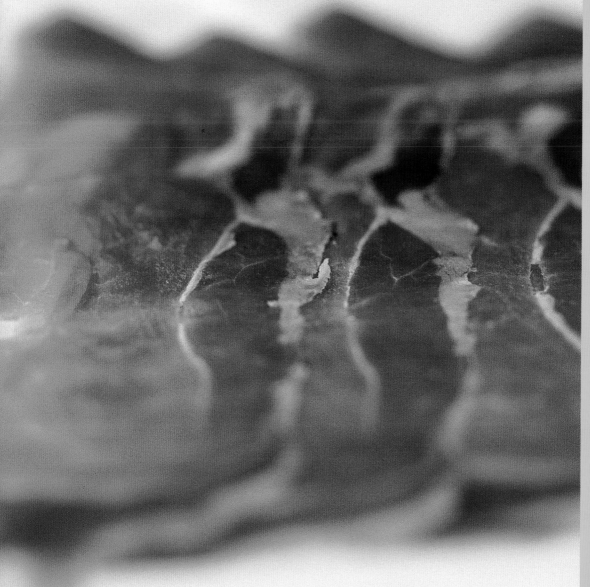

cod in prosciutto

Cod in prosciutto

Any firm white-fleshed fish can be cooked in this way. The outer covering of prosciutto or streaky bacon protects the fish and gives a good crisp texture. Simple, really. Serve with shredded cabbage and plenty of mash.

Trim the cod fillets into neat squares, season well and wrap in the prosciutto or bacon. Heat the oil in a fry pan and cook the fish on both sides until the prosciutto is lightly browned and the fish is cooked through, about 4 minutes each side, depending on thickness.

SERVES 4

4 cod fillets, around 180g each
sea salt
freshly ground black pepper
4 wide or 8 thin slices
   prosciutto, or rindless
   streaky bacon
1 tbsp olive oil
1/2 Savoy cabbage, around 500g
2 tbsp butter or olive oil
1 tbsp red wine vinegar
1 tsp caster sugar
1 tsp fennel or caraway seeds
few thyme sprigs or parsley
   leaves

Remove the outer cabbage leaves, cut out any core and finely shred the leaves. Cook in simmering salted water for 5 minutes – the cabbage should have a soft crunch but still retain a bright colour. Drain well, return to the dry pan and toss with the butter or olive oil, vinegar, sugar, fennel or caraway seeds, sea salt and pepper.

Spoon the cabbage onto four warmed dinner plates, place the pan-fried fish on top and scatter with the thyme or parsley.

Insalata di mare

I love the Italian way with a seafood salad – all relaxed, sunny and easy – using good-flavoured olive oil and simple herbs. Chickpeas aren't usually served with seafood, but I can't for the life of me think why not.

Scrub the mussels and pull out the beards, discarding any that don't close when sharply tapped. Rinse the squid well and cut the tubes into 4cm pieces. Score the insides lightly to help them curl.

Heat the olive oil, wine, peppercorns, garlic and parsley stems in a heavy lidded pan. Add the mussels, cover tightly and turn up the heat. Shake the pan after a minute or two, and take out any that have opened. Repeat twice, discarding any that don't open at all.

Strain the broth and return to the pan. Add the chickpeas and cook for 5 minutes. Add the squid and simmer for 1 minute or until just tender. Remove the squid and chickpeas with a slotted spoon and gently toss with the mussels, lemon juice, extra virgin olive oil, pepper and parsley. Add a spoonful or two of the seafood broth and serve warm or at room temperature, with lemon wedges.

SERVES 4
1 kg fresh mussels or clams
500 g cleaned small squid
(calamari)
2 tbsp olive oil
200 ml white wine
6 black peppercorns
2 garlic cloves, smashed
4 parsley stems
400 g canned chickpeas,
drained and rinsed
2 tbsp lemon juice
2 tbsp extra virgin olive oil
freshly ground black pepper
1 tbsp flat-leaf parsley
1 lemon, quartered

Goat cheese cannelloni

Rolling sheets of instant lasagne around a creamy cheese filling is a lot easier than stuffing cannelloni pasta tubes.

Heat the oven to 180°C/Gas 4. Bring a pot of salted water to the boil. Add the lasagne sheets, one at a time, and cook at a rolling boil until pliable, around 6 minutes. Drain and lay on a dry tea towel.

To make the filling, mash the ricotta, goat cheese, parsley, chives, salt, pepper and nutmeg together in a bowl.

Lay one sheet of lasagne on a board, spoon some of the mixture across the middle and roll into a cylinder. Place in a lightly greased baking dish. Repeat with the remaining lasagne and filling, laying the filled cannelloni side by side in the dish.

To make the sauce, whiz the tomatoes and their juice with the olive oil, sugar, and salt and pepper in a blender. Add the chopped herbs.

Pour the sauce over the cannelloni to cover completely. Scatter with parmesan and thyme, and bake for 30 minutes until bubbling hot.

SERVES 4

8 dried lasagne sheets

350g fresh ricotta cheese

100g soft, fresh goat cheese

2 tbsp finely chopped parsley

2 tsp finely snipped chives

$\frac{1}{2}$ tsp salt

$\frac{1}{2}$ tsp freshly ground black pepper

$\frac{1}{2}$ tsp ground nutmeg

2 tbsp finely grated parmesan

10 thyme sprigs

Sauce:

400g canned chopped tomatoes

1 tbsp olive oil

1 tsp sugar

1 tbsp chopped parsley

1 tbsp chopped thyme leaves

Beetroot rice

Whiz 3 cooked, peeled beetroot in a blender with sea salt and pepper. Heat a little butter in a fry pan and cook a finely chopped onion until soft. Add 300 g arborio (risotto) rice and stir well. Add 150 ml dry white wine, bubble it away, then add 1 litre hot chicken stock. Stir well, cover tightly and simmer gently for 15 minutes. Add the beetroot purée and cook for a few more minutes until the rice is tender. Add 2 tbsp freshly grated parmesan and serve.

onions

know your onions

Shallots are little red or brown onions with a milder, sweeter flavour – good for salads and fast-cooked dishes. They're easier to peel if you drop them in a pot of boiling water for 3 minutes first. Torpedo-shaped banana shallots are also milder – peel, cut into rings and lightly fry. The rest you know.

the onion-balsamic trick

For rich, sweet, and fast caramelised onions, heat 1 tbsp butter and 1 tbsp olive oil in a pan. When hot, fry 2 finely sliced onions for 10 minutes, tossing. Add 2 tbsp balsamic vinegar and cook for 5 minutes until crisp, but don't burn.

fast french onion soup

Fry 6 sliced white onions in 2 tbsp butter. Add 1 tbsp flour and cook for 1 to 2 minutes, then add 1.2 litres beef or chicken stock and simmer for 20 minutes. Top with grilled slices of sourdough bread, scatter with 3 tbsp grated gruyère cheese and place under the grill until the cheese bubbles.

one for the boys

Toss 3 finely sliced red onions in 2 tbsp olive oil and place on a baking tray. Top with 4 thick sliced plum tomatoes, and scatter with salt, pepper, thyme and rosemary. Lay 8 well-pricked, thick pork or beef sausages on top. Bake at 200°C/Gas 6 for 1 hour.

don't cry, baby

To cure onion tears, place onions in the freezer for 10 minutes before cutting, or chop them in the food processor.

sweet and sour onions

Gently simmer 30 small white onions with 2 tbsp tomato purée (paste), 100 ml red wine vinegar, 2 tbsp olive oil, 2 tbsp sugar, 1 bay leaf, 250 ml dry white wine, 250 ml water and 100 g raisins for 1 hour until tender. Serve with cold meats.

the nicest way to cook onions

Heat 1 tbsp butter, 2 tbsp olive oil, sea salt, 2 bay leaves, 100 ml dry white wine and 4 finely sliced onions in a pan. Cook very slowly for 45 minutes until meltingly soft. Serve as a sauce, to a roast leg of lamb or pork. Bliss.

how to roast onions

Don't peel, just cut them crosswise through the top as if quartering, but only halfway down. Drizzle with olive oil, scatter with thyme sprigs and bake at 180°C/Gas 4 for 1 hour for soft, sweet, irresistible onions.

the 15 minute dinner

Fry 2 chopped onions in a little butter and oil for 5 minutes. Add some chopped, leftover cooked ham, chicken or vegetables, and fry for 5 minutes. Stir in 3 eggs, salt, pepper and a pinch of cayenne, and cook until golden.

everyone loves onion rings

For crisp onion rings, submerge thickly sliced white onion rings in icy cold water for 1 hour. Drain and pat dry with paper towel, toss in flour and deep-fry. Serve with grilled fish, sausages, steaks and char-grilled veg.

Everything good starts with an onion. It gives a base of sweet

complexity, a bed for all the other flavours to lie on.

entertaining

Scallop stack

Beautiful, big, hand-dived scallops may be expensive, but they are worth it. Avoid scallops that have been soaked in water, as these will stew rather than sear, spoiling the dish. To turn this elegant starter into a main course, serve with lemony couscous.

Rinse and dry the scallops. Cut a cross in the base of the tomatoes and dunk them into a pot of boiling water for 20 seconds. Remove and peel. Cut in half, discard the juices and seeds, then cut the flesh into small dice.

Whisk the extra virgin olive oil and lemon juice in a bowl, with sea salt and pepper. Add the diced tomatoes, preserved lemon and basil or parsley. Toss lightly and set aside.

Heat the olive oil in a heavy-based fry pan and sear the scallops on one side, without moving, for 2 minutes, until crusty. Turn and cook on the other side for less than a minute, or until hot in the middle but still moist. Season well with sea salt and pepper.

Stack three scallops on each plate and drizzle with the tomato and lemon vinaigrette to serve.

SERVES 4

12 large sea scallops, cleaned

2 ripe red tomatoes

3 tbsp extra virgin olive oil

1 tbsp lemon juice, or more

sea salt

freshly ground black pepper

1 tbsp finely chopped
    preserved lemon

2 tbsp chopped basil or
    flat-leaf parsley

1 tbsp olive oil

Thai seafood soup

'Dtom yam gung' is the most famous of all Thai soups, for its provocative balance of chilli, lime juice and fish sauce. Making the stock from the prawn heads gives that authentic touch of 'red oil' to the broth.

Peel and devein the prawns, saving the heads and shells. Heat the oil in a heavy-based fry pan, add the prawn heads and shells, and toss well over a fairly high heat, then crush with a potato masher to extract the juices. Add the boiling water and simmer for 10 minutes.

Finely slice the chilli and mushrooms. Strain the prawn stock through a sieve into a saucepan, discarding the heads and shells. Add the lemongrass, chilli, mushrooms and lime leaves, and simmer for 5 minutes. Add the prawns, sugar and fish sauce, and simmer for a couple of minutes until the prawns turn pink.

Remove from the heat, add the lime juice and half the coriander, and taste for the balance between hot, sweet and sour flavours. Serve in four deep soup bowls, scattered with the remaining coriander.

SERVES 4

8 to 12 medium raw prawns in shell
1 tbsp vegetable oil
1 litre boiling water
1 small red chilli
150g button mushrooms or straw mushrooms
2 lemongrass stalks, white part only, bashed
4 kaffir lime leaves
1 tbsp sugar
2 tbsp Thai fish sauce
3 tbsp lime juice, or more to taste
3 tbsp coriander leaves

saffron cream mussels

Saffron cream mussels

A touch of saffron and curry powder in the creamy sauce makes these mussels irresistible. Cook the mussels lightly so they are plump, sweet and still full of their own juices.

Discard any broken mussels, and those that do not close when sharply tapped. Scrub the mussels well and pull out the little beards. Put the white wine, onion and garlic in a heavy lidded fry pan, bring to the boil and boil for 1 minute. Add the mussels, cover tightly and cook for 1 minute.

Shake the pan and remove any mussels that have opened, then repeat the process, keeping the opened mussels in a covered bowl. Discard any mussels that remain closed. Strain the cooking broth into a jug and set aside.

Melt the butter in a small saucepan, scatter on the flour and cook, stirring, for about 3 minutes. Gradually pour in the mussel broth, stirring constantly, then slowly pour in the milk, stirring.

Beat the egg yolk, curry powder, saffron, turmeric and cream together, then add to the sauce, stirring well; don't let it boil.

Remove the top shells of about half the mussels, and discard. Pile all the mussels into four warmed shallow bowls and pour the sauce over the top to serve.

SERVES 4

1.5kg mussels
125ml dry white wine
1 small onion, finely chopped
1 garlic clove, finely chopped
1 tbsp butter
1 tbsp plain flour
100ml milk
1 egg yolk
$\frac{1}{2}$ tsp mild curry powder
$\frac{1}{2}$ tsp powdered saffron
$\frac{1}{2}$ tsp ground turmeric
100ml double cream or
    whipping cream

Red mullet with laksa sauce

Singaporean laksa is usually a soup with noodles, but I've borrowed the rich, creamy sauce for a special dinner. Keep a jar of curry laksa paste on hand and it's made in 10 minutes. Do it again with salmon, bream, or even prawns, chicken or vegetables, and serve with rice or noodles.

Peel the cucumber and slice it as finely as you can. Salt the cucumber and set aside.

To make the sauce, heat the oil in a fry pan or wok. Add the curry laksa paste and fry for 3 or 4 minutes until fragrant. Add the chicken stock, salt and sugar and bring to the boil. Reduce to a simmer and add the coconut milk, stirring constantly. Simmer uncovered for 5 minutes until lightly creamy.

To cook the fish, heat the oil in a non-stick fry pan and cook the fillets, skin-side down, for 2 to 3 minutes, gently pressing them into the pan to help crisp the skin. Turn and cook the other side for 1 minute. Season with salt and pepper.

Lightly rinse the cucumber, and pat dry. Place in the centre of four warmed shallow pasta bowls and top with the red mullet.

Add the lime juice to the hot sauce, and ladle it around the fish. Top with coriander leaves and serve.

SERVES 4

1 cucumber
2 tsp fine salt
1 tbsp vegetable oil
4 red mullet fillets, around
160 g each
sea salt
freshly ground black pepper
handful of coriander leaves

Sauce:
1 tbsp vegetable oil
1 tbsp curry laksa paste
(eg Reuben Solomon's) or
Thai red curry paste
150 ml chicken stock or water
$1/2$ tsp salt
1 tbsp soft brown sugar
400 ml coconut milk
1 tbsp lime juice

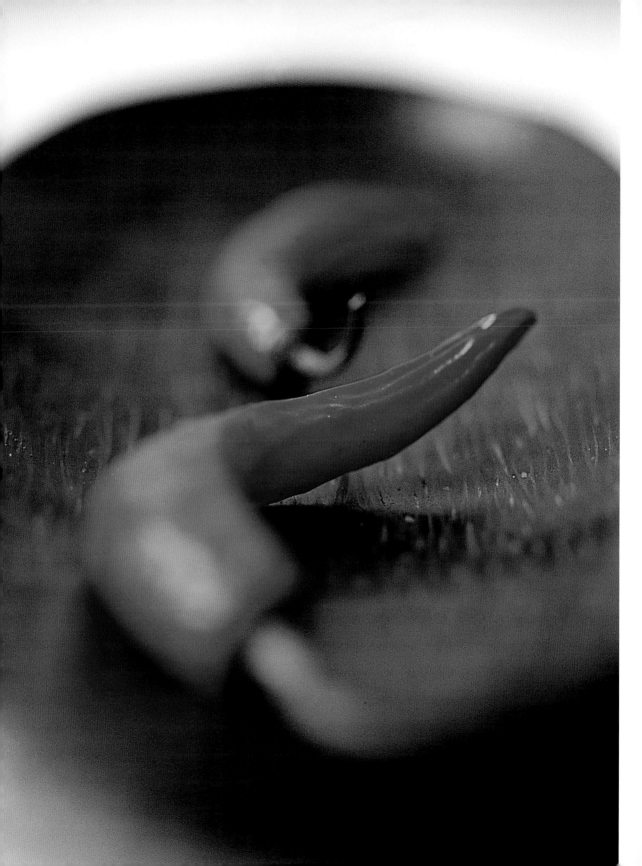

Chilli basil mussels

Enticing, invigorating, exciting and exotic, this is a great dish of Thai flavours for mussel lovers.

Scrub the mussels well, pulling out the little beards, and discard any that do not close when sharply tapped. Pick the basil and mint leaves from their stems.

Heat the oil in a wok, and stir-fry the garlic and ginger for just 30 seconds. Carefully add the wine and boil for 30 seconds, then add the fish sauce, chillies and half the mussels. Cover and steam for 1 minute, shake the pan, then remove the opened mussels. Do this another two or three times, then discard any mussels that don't open. Repeat with remaining mussels.

Bring the broth to the boil, and add the chilli sauce and most of the basil and mint leaves, stirring. Return the mussels to the pan, briefly tossing well over high heat. Scatter with the remaining basil and mint to serve.

SERVES 4

2kg mussels

bunch of basil

bunch of mint

2 tbsp vegetable oil

3 garlic cloves, peeled and smashed

1 tbsp finely chopped fresh ginger

125ml dry white wine

2 tbsp Thai fish sauce

2 red chillies, finely chopped

3 tbsp sweet, seedy Thai chilli sauce

sweet and sour sauce

Sweet and sour fish

If you have been put off sweet-and-sour by the Chinese take-away cliché of glutinous, sickly sweet, crimson sauce, try this sweetly sharp version instead. It is a lot closer to the original Shanghainese recipe, and makes the flavour of the fish jump in your mouth.

SERVES 4

200g bean sprouts

4 tbsp vegetable oil

4 thick white fish fillets (eg hake, haddock, cod, snapper), around 180g each

2 tbsp cornflour to coat

2 spring onions, finely sliced

Sauce:

6 dried Chinese mushrooms

5cm knob fresh root ginger

2 tsp cornflour

3 tbsp rice vinegar or wine vinegar

2 tbsp caster sugar

2 tbsp tomato ketchup

1/2 tsp salt

1 tbsp soy sauce

1 tbsp rice wine or dry sherry

200ml water or chicken stock

Put the dried mushrooms for the sauce in a bowl of boiling water and leave to soak for 30 minutes. Peel and slice the ginger, then cut into very fine matchsticks.

To make the sauce, drain and finely slice the mushrooms, discarding the stems. Mix the cornflour and vinegar to a paste. Place in a small saucepan with the sugar, tomato ketchup, salt, soy sauce, rice wine, water and mushrooms. Bring to the boil, stirring until the sauce is thick and glossy.

Rinse the bean sprouts and shake dry. Heat half the oil in a fry pan. Add the ginger and fry for 1 minute, stirring, then lift out with a slotted spoon and add to the sauce. Fry the bean sprouts in the pan for 30 seconds, then divide among four warmed dinner plates.

Coat the fish fillets lightly with cornflour. Heat the remaining oil in the pan and fry the fish fillets for around 3 minutes on each side until golden. Place on the bean sprouts and spoon the hot sauce over the top. Scatter with spring onions and serve, with rice or noodles.

Salmon, bacon and peas

Salmon is the little black dress of home entertaining, able to be as formal or casual as you like. Swap the peas for a green salad or char-grilled vegetables accordingly.

Wrap each salmon fillet in a rasher of bacon. Finely chop the rest of the bacon and the onion.

Heat half the olive oil in a fry pan and cook the onion for 5 minutes, then add the chopped bacon and cook gently for 10 minutes until the onion is soft and translucent.

Cook the peas in simmering salted water for 5 minutes or until tender. Drain and refresh under cold running water. Drain well and add to the bacon and onion with pepper to taste. Reheat gently.

Heat the remaining oil in a non-stick frying pan and sear the salmon for 2 to 3 minutes on each side until the bacon is crisp and the salmon is still pink in the centre. Spoon the peas and bacon onto warmed plates, top with the salmon and serve.

SERVES 4

4 salmon fillets, around
180g each
8 rashers rindless streaky
bacon or pancetta
1 onion, peeled
2 tbsp olive oil
450g podded fresh or
frozen peas
sea salt
freshly ground black pepper

Salmon in cabbage

An elegant way to serve an elegant fish for a dinner party or special meal. Easy, too, because you can package up the salmon beforehand, ready for steaming when you want to eat.

Peel off and discard the outer leaves of the cabbage, then carefully peel off 4 good, bright coloured leaves. Drop them into a pot of simmering, salted water for 3 minutes, then drain and rinse under cold water. Shave off any inner ribs on the blanched leaves.

Trim the salmon fillets into neat squares, and remove any pin bones. Spread out a sheet of cling film on a work surface and lay a blanched cabbage leaf on top. Place a salmon fillet in the middle, season well, and gently wrap the leaf around it to make a parcel. Wrap the parcel tightly in the cling film. Repeat to make the remaining parcels, and chill.

SERVES 4

1 firm Savoy cabbage

4 salmon fillets, around 180g each, and 3cm thick

sea salt

freshly ground black pepper

2 tomatoes

2 tbsp extra virgin olive oil

1 tbsp tiny capers, rinsed

1 lemon, quartered

Cut the tomatoes in half, and squeeze out and discard the seeds and juice. Finely chop the flesh.

Fill the base of your steamer with water and bring to the boil. Carefully remove the cling film from the cabbage parcels, place them in the steamer, cover tightly and cook for 8 to 10 minutes.

Gently warm the chopped tomatoes, extra virgin olive oil and capers in a pan. Place the cabbage parcels on warmed plates and spoon the tomato salsa over and around them. Serve with lemon wedges and small boiled potatoes.

Teriyaki salmon

Japan's brilliant way with steak also suits the healthy richness of salmon. Serve on a mangetout (snow pea) salad for a really crisp, fresh bite.

To make the teriyaki sauce, combine the sugar, sake, mirin and soy sauce in a bowl, and set aside.

Wash and dry the mangetout, trim if necessary, then finely slice lengthwise into matchsticks, using the tip of a sharp knife. Mix the rice wine vinegar and sesame oil together in a bowl, add the mangetout and toss until coated.

Remove any pin bones from the salmon fillets and pat dry with paper towel. Heat the vegetable oil in a heavy non-stick fry pan. Cook the fillets, skin-side down, for around 2 minutes or until the skin is crisp and you can see the flesh gradually changing colour.

Turn the fillets and add most of the teriyaki sauce to the pan. Allow the sauce to bubble up around the salmon as you cook the other side for about 3 minutes, leaving the middle pink. (Don't allow to boil dry, or the sugar will burn.)

Divide the mangetout between plates and arrange the salmon fillets on top. Quickly heat the remaining teriyaki sauce and spoon it over the salmon to serve.

SERVES 4
250 g mangetout (snow peas)
1 tbsp rice wine vinegar, or white wine vinegar
2 tsp sesame oil
4 salmon fillets with skin, around 180 g each
1 tbsp vegetable oil

Teriyaki sauce:
1 tbsp sugar
3 tbsp sake (Japanese rice wine)
2 tbsp mirin (sweet rice wine), or sweet sherry
3 tbsp soy sauce

Swordfish with courgettes

Seared swordfish gets dressed up with courgettes (zucchini) and a lemony, herby Mediterranean dressing, known as salmoriglio. This is a great way to serve fresh tuna steaks too.

Trim the courgettes, discarding the ends, then grate coarsely. Heat 2 tbsp olive oil in a non-stick fry pan and add the courgettes with sea salt and black pepper. Toss well over a medium heat for 2 to 3 minutes until softened.

Heat 1 tbsp olive oil in a non-stick fry pan. When hot, season the swordfish well and sear on one side until quite golden, about 3 minutes. Turn and cook the other side for another 2 minutes, depending on the thickness.

To make the dressing, whisk the lemon juice, olive oil and sea salt in a bowl, and stir in the parsley, oregano and capers.

Arrange the swordfish on a bed of courgettes and top with a caper berry or a few extra capers. Serve the dressing in a bowl, to be spooned on top.

SERVES 4

4 medium courgettes
(zucchini)
3 tbsp olive oil
sea salt
freshly ground black pepper
6 swordfish steaks, around
180g each
4 caper berries, or a few
extra capers

Salmoriglio dressing:
2 tbsp lemon juice
6 tbsp extra virgin olive oil
1/2 tsp sea salt
2 tbsp parsley leaves
2 tsp oregano leaves
2 tbsp capers, rinsed

Duck with beetroot

Duck breasts don't have to be undercooked inside and over-scorched outside. Gently steaming them before pan-frying to crisp and colour the skin makes it easy – for both you and the duck to get it right.

Cook the unpeeled beetroot in boiling water until tender – this can take up to 1 hour, but at least you don't have much to do. Drain, reserving 200 ml of the water. Rinse the beetroot under cold running water and rub off the skins and stems, then cut into small dice.

Return the beetroot to the pan. Add the reserved liquid, vinegar, sugar, salt and pepper. Bring to the boil, stirring, and allow to bubble until the liquid is reduced to a slightly sticky syrup. Keep warm.

Meanwhile, wash and dry the duck breasts, and score the skin in a criss-cross pattern, with a sharp knife. Rub with the salt and thyme leaves. Place on a heatproof plate that will fit into your steamer and steam over simmering water for 20 minutes. Remove the duck breasts and pat dry. (You can prepare to this stage a few hours ahead.)

Heat the oil in a non-stick frying pan and sear the duck breasts, skin-side down, until the skin is crisp and golden. Turn them over, reduce the heat, and cook gently until heated through.

Carve each duck breast thickly on the diagonal, and serve with the beetroot and a leafy green salad.

SERVES 4

4 duck breasts with skin,
  around 200g each
1/2 tsp salt
1 tbsp thyme sprigs
2 tsp olive oil

Beetroot:
4 medium beetroot
50 ml white vinegar
150g caster sugar
1 tsp salt
1/2 tsp freshly ground
  black pepper

Chilli orange duck

Here is a nice twist on duck à l'orange – aromatic, crisp-skinned duck in a sticky, sweet and spicy citrus syrup that glows on the plate.

Scrub the oranges well. Cut the rind from 2 oranges, using a sharp knife, and trim off most of the pith. Cut the rind into short, thin strips. Squeeze the juice from the oranges – you need 250 ml.

Combine the orange rind and juice, sugar, ginger, chilli, star anise, cinnamon sticks, sweet chilli sauce, fish sauce, vinegar and red wine in a saucepan and bring to the boil, stirring. Boil for around 10 minutes, stirring occasionally, until lightly syrupy.

Prick the duck skin well, and heat the oil in a non-stick fry pan. Add the duck breasts and sear, skin-side down, for 8 minutes until browned, then turn and cook for another 8 minutes. Rest for 5 minutes before serving.

Cut the spring onions into finger lengths, then into strips. Slice the duck thickly, arrange on warmed plates and scatter with spring onion shreds. Spoon the sauce over the top, with the spices – for atmosphere, not for eating. Serve with rice or noodles.

SERVES 4

2–3 oranges

100g sugar

1 tbsp grated fresh ginger

1 small red chilli, finely sliced

2 star anise

2 cinnamon sticks

1 tbsp sweet chilli sauce

1 tbsp Thai fish sauce

1 tbsp rice wine vinegar, or
   other wine vinegar

2 tbsp red wine or port

4 duck breasts, around
   200g each

1 tbsp vegetable oil

2 spring onions, trimmed

Pancetta chicken

Wash and pat dry 8 large, boned chicken thighs. Mix
1 tbsp grated lemon rind with 2 crushed garlic cloves,
2 tbsp chopped parsley, sea salt and pepper, and rub
into the inside of each thigh. Roll up and wrap in slices
of pancetta or thin bacon. Bake at 180°C/Gas 4 for
45 minutes or until tender. Serve on buttered sweetcorn.

Beef with shallots

My friends tell me that every time they cook this, their guests say it's just like eating in a restaurant. It is better than that, though. Restaurants don't give you second helpings of mash.

Cook the unpeeled shallots in simmering water for 5 minutes, then drain and peel.

Heat the grill, or a cast-iron grill pan or fry pan, until hot. Rub the beef with 1 tbsp olive oil, sea salt and pepper. Grill or pan-sear the beef on all sides until well marked, but still rare inside, around 12 minutes. Remove from the heat and allow to rest for 10 minutes.

In the meantime, cook the potatoes in a pan of simmering salted water until tender.

Heat the remaining 1 tbsp olive oil in a fry pan, and fry the shallots for about 10 minutes until golden. Add the balsamic vinegar, thyme and rosemary sprigs, and cook gently, stirring as the shallots colour and caramelise.

Gently heat the milk with the smashed garlic until hot. Drain the potatoes and mash well, then beat in the milk, discarding the garlic.

Discard the string, slice the beef into 1cm thick slices and season with salt and pepper. Spoon the mash onto warmed plates and arrange the beef on top with the caramelised shallots. Scatter with parsley or chervil to serve.

SERVES 4

20 small brown shallots
600g rolled fillet of beef, tied with string
2 tbsp extra virgin olive oil
sea salt
freshly ground black pepper
600g red-skinned potatoes, peeled
2 tbsp balsamic vinegar
few thyme and rosemary sprigs
125ml milk
2 garlic cloves, peeled and smashed
parsley or chervil sprigs, to serve

Rare beef with Thai herbs

The next time you want to 'do something special', go and buy a big, beautiful piece of beef. It's an event, a celebration, and best of all, it rests for an hour before serving so you can do everything in advance. Add a zingy dressing of herbs, chilli, fish sauce and lime juice, and serve it forth to the multitudes.

Place the beef in a shallow dish, rub with the soy sauce and sesame oil, and leave to marinate for a few hours or overnight.

Heat the oven to 220°C/Gas 7. Heat the vegetable oil in a heavy fry pan and sear the beef until browned and crusty all over.

Transfer the seared beef to a lightly oiled roasting tray and roast for 15 minutes. Reduce the setting to 180°C/Gas 4 and cook for a further 25 to 30 minutes, for rare to medium rare. Remove and rest the beef under a loose sheet of foil for an hour before carving.

To make the dressing, whisk the lime juice, fish sauce, sesame oil and sugar together until the sugar has dissolved. Add the shallots, chilli, spring onions and herb leaves, and toss well.

Slice the beef, discarding the string, and arrange on a serving platter. Spoon the dressing over the beef and serve, with lime wedges.

SERVES 6 TO 8

1 kg fillet of beef, rolled and tied
2 tbsp soy sauce
1 tbsp sesame oil
2 tbsp vegetable oil
2 limes, quartered

Dressing:
2 tbsp lime juice
2 tbsp Thai fish sauce or soy sauce
1 tbsp sesame oil
2 tsp sugar
4 small red shallots, finely sliced
1 small red chilli, finely sliced
2 spring onions, finely sliced
handful of basil leaves
handful of mint leaves
handful of coriander leaves

steak with mushrooms

Steak with mushrooms

A rich and creamy mushroom sauce smothers pan-seared steaks in a sort of beef stroganoff for the 21st century.

Cut the onion in half and slice finely. Wipe the mushrooms, discard the stalks and slice finely.

Melt the butter with the olive oil in a non-stick fry pan, and gently cook the onion for 5 minutes. Add the mushrooms and cook for 5 minutes. Add white wine, sea salt, pepper and paprika, and bring to the boil, stirring. Reduce the heat and simmer for 5 minutes.

Heat a cast-iron grill pan or another heavy non-stick fry pan. Brush the steaks with a little olive oil and cook on one side, without moving, for 2 minutes. Season, turn, and cook for 2 to 3 minutes for medium rare. Season again, and leave to rest in a warm place.

Add the sour cream, mustard, tomato purée and most of the parsley to the mushrooms and cook, stirring, for 5 minutes. Place the steaks on warmed plates, spoon the mushroom sauce on top and scatter with the remaining chopped parsley.

SERVES 4

1 onion, peeled

500g mushrooms

1 tbsp butter

1 tbsp olive oil

125ml white wine

sea salt

freshly ground black pepper

1 tsp sweet paprika

4 rump steaks, around 200g
   each, and 2.5cm thick

3 tbsp sour cream or crème
   fraîche

1 tsp Dijon mustard

1 tbsp tomato purée (paste)

1 tbsp finely chopped parsley

Grilled lamb and beans

The best way to get great looking lamb chops is to buy a well-trimmed rack of lamb and divide it into 4 double chops.

Heat the oven to 180°C/Gas 4. Toss the cherry tomatoes and garlic cloves in 1 tbsp olive oil in a small roasting pan, and bake for 30 minutes.

Heat a cast-iron grill pan, or the grill, until hot. Cut the rack of lamb into 4 double chops, and swipe them in the hot oil of the roasting tomatoes. Grill, skin-side down for 3 minutes, then for around 2 to 3 minutes on either side for medium rare, depending on size.

Drain and rinse the canned beans. Heat them gently with the remaining 2 tbsp extra virgin olive oil, sea salt, black pepper and chopped parsley. Divide between warmed plates.

Cut each chop in two or leave whole if you prefer, and arrange on the beans. Quickly toss the roasted tomatoes and garlic with the basil and spoon around the chops. Squeeze out the soft garlic from the skins to eat with the lamb.

SERVES 4

200g cherry tomatoes

4 garlic cloves, lightly smashed

3 tbsp extra virgin olive oil

1 x 8-chop rack of lamb (well trimmed)

400g canned white beans (cannellini or flageolet)

sea salt

freshly ground black pepper

2 tbsp finely chopped parsley

handful of basil leaves

Slashed roast lamb

Lamb slashed almost to the bone cooks faster, remains tender and looks spectacular. You'll end up with chunky slices coated in a garlicky, lemony seasoning that are a joy to eat. Serve with potatoes roasted in the same pan, and a green salad.

Heat oven to 220°C/Gas 7. Holding the leg of lamb with its meatiest side towards you, slash 5 times almost to the bone, at 2.5cm intervals.

Combine the parsley, garlic, anchovies, capers, lemon rind and breadcrumbs in a bowl. Mix in the olive oil to make a paste and push between the lamb slices. Re-shape the meat and tie with string.

Scatter with rosemary, drizzle with a little olive oil and bake for 20 minutes. Reduce setting to 190°C/Gas 5 and bake for another 45 minutes to 1 hour. Leave to rest under foil for 10 minutes.

Strain the juices into a bowl and spoon off surface fat. Remove string and carve across the lamb, parallel to the bone. Arrange on warm plates, drizzle with the juices and serve, with lemon wedges.

SERVES 4 TO 6

1 leg of lamb, around 2kg
3 tbsp roughly chopped parsley
4 garlic cloves, chopped
2 anchovies, chopped
2 tbsp salted capers, rinsed
1 tbsp coarsely grated lemon rind
4 tbsp soft fresh breadcrumbs
3 tbsp extra virgin olive oil
4 rosemary sprigs
extra olive oil to drizzle
1 lemon, quartered

Roast tamari veg

Tamari is a Japanese wheat-free soy sauce with a deeper, more complex flavour than your standard soy. Use normal soy if you don't have it.

Heat the oven to 200°C/Gas 6. Cut the pumpkin into thinnish wedges, cut off the skin, and discard the seeds. Wash the carrots, peel and trim the tops neatly. Peel the parsnips and cut lengthwise into quarters. Peel and halve the beetroot.

SERVES 4

500g pumpkin

2 bunches of baby carrots

4 parsnips

4 fresh beetroot

2 tbsp tamari, or soy sauce

2 tbsp extra virgin olive oil

$\frac{1}{2}$ tsp sea salt

$\frac{1}{2}$ tsp freshly ground black
pepper

handful of coriander leaves

Dressing:

2 tbsp rice wine vinegar, or
white wine vinegar

1 tbsp Thai fish sauce

3 tbsp extra virgin olive oil

1 tbsp sugar

Combine the tamari, olive oil, sea salt and pepper in a big bowl, add the vegetables and toss until well coated. Tip into a baking tray and bake for 45 minutes to 1 hour until tender and nicely browned.

To make the dressing, whisk the rice wine vinegar, fish sauce, olive oil and sugar together in a bowl. Drizzle over the vegetables, jumble everything up a bit and pile high on warmed serving plates. Scatter with coriander to serve.

Asparagus and pea soup

As with any green vegetable soup, I suggest whizzing a handful of fresh flat-leaf parsley into the finished soup just before serving, to intensify the freshness and the colour. And don't feel you have to stand a spear of asparagus in the soup as I did for the photograph here. All cooks have their own ways of amusing themselves, and this was mine.

Wash the asparagus, then bend the spears until they snap and discard the woody ends. Finely chop the asparagus, reserving the tips for serving.

Bring the chicken stock to the boil, add the asparagus and green peas and simmer for 15 minutes until soft. Add sea salt and pepper and taste.

Cool the soup a little, then purée in the blender or food processor in batches. Add the parsley leaves to the last batch, and whiz.

To serve, gently reheat the soup and the asparagus tips for about 5 minutes, then ladle into four warmed soup bowls. I don't think it needs cream, but you could add a spoonful or two when reheating if you're feeling creamy.

SERVES 6

1 kg thick asparagus

1.2 litres chicken stock

250 g podded fresh or
    frozen peas

sea salt

freshly ground black pepper

handful of flat-leaf parsley
    leaves

herbs

bite into a fresh herb sandwich
Finely snip a handful of chives and mix with some finely chopped mint, parsley and thyme. Sandwich between slices of fresh white bread, spread with cream cheese or fresh ricotta spiked with sea salt and black pepper.

add fresh mint to your salad greens
Add a handful of fresh mint leaves to your next green leaf salad, dress it with 2 tbsp extra virgin olive oil, 1 tbsp red wine vinegar, sea salt, pepper and 1 tsp Dijon mustard, and every mouthful will taste wild.

add fragrance to fruit
Fruits love herbs, not just spices. Add basil to fresh ripe peaches and pineapple. Chop fresh mint and papaya and toss with a squeeze of lime juice and a little sugar. Poach stone fruit in a light sugar syrup with bay leaves and peppercorns.

a simple way with sage
Fry sage leaves in olive oil until crisp, then remove. Use the oil to pan-fry mushrooms, potatoes, crumbed veal, pork chops or duck breasts. Serve topped with the crisp-fried sage leaves.

give the knife a rest
You don't always have to chop fresh herbs. Chives are better snipped with scissors, and basil leaves are better simply torn. Throw whole parsley, sage and oregano leaves into pasta sauces, soups and stews, and strew whole sprigs of thyme and rosemary over roasts.

add a herb crust to fish
Mix 2 tbsp chopped basil, parsley and chervil with a cupful of soft breadcrumbs, salt, pepper, a pinch of cayenne and a squeeze of lime juice. Dip 4 fish fillets into beaten egg, then into the herb crumbs, and fry until crisp and golden.

marinate everything in sight
Marinate lamb chops with rosemary or oregano in olive oil before grilling. Marinate chicken in coriander, mint, basil and vegetable oil before barbecuing. Marinate sliced tomatoes and goat cheese in thyme, garlic and olive oil, and serve all summer long.

bay-leaf your meatballs
Make your favourite bite-sized meatballs, wrap a lightly oiled bay leaf around each one and secure with a wooden cocktail stick or toothpick. Bake and serve, but don't eat the leaf.

zap your potato salad
Chives are the obvious pick, but try spiking potato salad with a gremolata – 2 crushed garlic cloves tossed with 2 tbsp finely chopped parsley and 1 tbsp grated lemon rind – and prepare to be amazed. Scatter the same gremolata over pan-fried fish, parmesan risotto, roast chicken, and baked mushrooms.

make a pot of herb tea
Add boiling water to a handful of crushed mint or basil, or a few stems of bashed lemongrass and leave to steep for 5 minutes. Strain and serve with a sprig of the same herb.

Variety isn't the spice of life, after all – it's the herb. Change the herb and you alter the smell, the taste and the look of your food. Simple, really.

suppers

Spicy pork noodles

This is the Chinese equivalent of spaghetti Bolognese. Brown bean sauce is available from Asian food stores.

Mix the brown bean sauce, hoisin, soy sauce, water and sugar together in a bowl, stirring. Set aside.

Peel the cucumber, and pare lengthwise with a vegetable peeler into ribbons. Cut the ribbons into matchsticks and set aside.

Heat a wok or fry pan. When hot, add the oil and stir-fry most of the spring onions for 30 seconds. Add the pork and stir-fry for a few minutes until browned. Add the sauce mix and stir-fry for about 5 minutes until the water has evaporated, oil rises to the surface, and the pork smells sweet and spicy. Mix the cornflour with the water or rice wine, and add to the meat, stirring.

Place the noodles in a large heatproof bowl and cover with a kettleful of boiling water. Drain well and return to the bowl. Add the spicy pork sauce and toss well. Divide between four deep warmed bowls, scatter with cucumber and spring onions and serve with chopsticks.

SERVES 4

1 tbsp brown bean or chilli
   bean sauce
1 tbsp hoisin sauce
2 tbsp soy sauce
125 ml water
1 tsp soft brown sugar
½ cucumber
2 tbsp peanut oil
4 spring onions, finely chopped
500 g minced pork
1 tbsp cornflour
1 tbsp water or Chinese rice
   wine
500 g fresh oiled egg noodles
   (Hokkien)

Long life noodles

Cantonese legend has it that the longer the noodle, the longer you will live. Or it could just be that noodles are good for you.

Put the dried mushrooms in a bowl, pour on the boiling water and soak for at least 30 minutes. Cut the white leek into 5cm lengths, halve lengthwise, then cut into very thin matchstick strips.

Lift the mushrooms from the water, discard the stems and slice the caps finely; set aside. Strain 100 ml of the soaking water into a bowl and stir in the soy sauce, oyster sauce, sesame oil and sugar; set aside. Place the noodles in a large heatproof bowl and pour a kettleful of boiling water over the top, then drain well.

Heat the wok. When hot, add the oil and stir-fry the ginger and garlic for 1 minute. Add the leek and mushrooms, tossing well over a high heat. Add the sauce, bring to the boil and cook, stirring, for 1 minute.

Add the tofu and cook for 1 minute. Add the noodles, and cook for about 2 minutes, tossing, until they have absorbed most of the sauce. Scatter with spring onions and serve with chopsticks.

SERVES 4

6 dried Chinese mushrooms
200 ml boiling water
1 leek, white part only
2 tbsp soy sauce
1 tbsp oyster sauce
1 tsp sesame oil
1 tsp sugar
450 g fresh oiled egg noodles (Hokkien)
1 tbsp vegetable oil
1 tbsp grated fresh root ginger
2 garlic cloves, crushed
200 g tofu, drained and cut into cubes
2 spring onions, finely sliced

chilli soy tofu

Chilli soy tofu

Even if you don't like tofu, you'll like this tofu. Serve with rice for a light, simple supper for two, or team it with the Asian omelette on page 267, or stir-fry duck noodles opposite, for a more substantial supper for four.

Fill the base of your steamer with water and bring to the boil.

Drain the tofu and place it on a heatproof plate that will fit inside the steamer. Steam the tofu for 20 minutes, then drain off excess water and carefully transfer to a serving plate.

Finely slice the red chilli. Trim and finely slice the spring onions.

Heat the soy sauce, sesame oil and oyster sauce together in a small pan until hot. Pour the mixture over the tofu, scatter with red chilli, spring onion and coriander leaves, and serve.

SERVES 2

500g pack fresh tofu

1 small red chilli

2 spring onions

3 tbsp soy sauce

2 tsp sesame oil

1 tsp oyster sauce

2 tbsp coriander leaves

Stir-fry duck noodles

Oiled egg noodles, also known as Hokkien or stir-fry noodles, look like fat golden spaghetti. Oriental food stores and larger supermarkets sell them. Pick up barbecued roast duck from Chinatown, or use leftover duck or barbecued chicken.

Remove the meat from the duck and finely slice it, discarding the bones. Finely chop the spring onions, celery and chilli.

Heat a wok or fry pan, add the oil and heat. Add the ginger and garlic and cook until golden to flavour the oil, then remove and discard. Add the celery, chilli and half the spring onions and stir-fry for 2 minutes. Add the duck and stir-fry for 1 minute.

Put the noodles in a heatproof bowl, cover with boiling water, then drain immediately. Add to the wok and toss well over high heat.

Add the bean sprouts, toss, then add the rice wine. Add the hoi sin, oyster and soy sauces, and toss well. Scatter with the remaining spring onions and serve.

SERVES 4

½ roast duck (eg Chinese barbecued roast duck)

3 spring onions

2 celery stalks

1 small red chilli

2 tbsp vegetable oil

1 slice fresh ginger

1 garlic clove, peeled and smashed

400g fresh oiled egg noodles

200g bean sprouts, rinsed

1 tbsp Chinese rice wine, or dry sherry

1 tbsp hoi sin sauce

2 tbsp oyster sauce

2 tbsp soy sauce

Asian omelette

This works well with leftover roast pork, or barbecued Chinese char sieu pork from Chinatown. It is also delicious with cooked prawns or crabmeat instead of the meat.

Finely slice the roast pork. Rinse the bean sprouts in boiling water and drain. Wash the watercress, and shake dry.

To make one omelette, crack 2 eggs into a small bowl, and lightly beat in 1 tbsp rice wine, salt, pepper and $\frac{1}{2}$ tsp sesame oil.

Heat 1 tbsp vegetable oil in a hot wok over high heat, swirling it around to coat the entire surface. Pour in the beaten eggs and quickly swirl to form an even omelette. Cook for 2 to 3 minutes until the egg is firm, then lower the heat.

Arrange some roast pork in the centre, top with bean sprouts and watercress, and cook gently for a further 2 or 3 minutes.

Loosen the edges with a knife, then gently slide the omelette onto a warm plate, folding it over. Keep it warm while you make three more omelettes. Drizzle with oyster sauce to serve.

SERVES 4

450g boneless roast or
barbecued pork
400g bean sprouts
200g watercress
8 large free-range eggs
4 tbsp Chinese rice wine,
or dry sherry
sea salt
freshly ground black pepper
2 tsp sesame oil
4 tbsp vegetable oil
4 tbsp oyster or hoi sin sauce

blue cheese potato

Onions with cheese

Everyone who loves baked onions calls this a great supper. Those who quite like them call it a great side dish for lamb, chicken or steak.

Heat the oven to 180°C/Gas 4. Peel the onions and arrange them in a lightly oiled baking tray so that they fit snugly side by side.

Drizzle with the olive oil and bake for 1 hour until soft. Remove from the oven, and turn the heat to 220°C/Gas 7.

Combine the grated parmesan, nutmeg, sea salt, black pepper and cream in a jug or bowl, stirring well.

Pour the cream over the baked onions, and sprinkle with paprika. Return the dish to the oven for about 15 minutes until the cheese sauce is golden brown and bubbling. Let stand for a minute or two before serving.

SERVES 4

8 medium white onions

2 tbsp olive oil

4 tbsp freshly grated parmesan

pinch of freshly grated nutmeg

sea salt

freshly ground black pepper

250ml single or whipping
  cream

½ tsp smoked paprika

Blue cheese potato

Put the spuds in the oven just before you go out for a quick drink or an evening meeting, return an hour or so later and supper is almost done.

Heat the oven to 200°C/Gas 6. Scrub the potatoes well and dry thoroughly. Prick lightly, coat in olive oil, and roll in salt and pepper.

Place the potatoes on the rack in the centre of the oven and bake for 1¹/₂ to 2 hours, until soft to the touch. (If you can hear them softly whistle, they're perfect.)

Fry the bacon in a non-stick fry pan until crisp, drain well on paper towel, and chop or crumble into shards.

Cut a cross in the top of each potato, and push in at the edges to expose the inside. Pile the sour cream and blue cheese on top, scatter with bacon and chives, and serve before it all melts.

SERVES 4
4 large baking potatoes
(eg King Edward), around
250 g each
1 tbsp olive oil
1 tsp sea salt
freshly ground black pepper
4 rashers streaky bacon
150 g sour cream or
crème fraîche
150 g gorgonzola or Roquefort,
crumbled
2 tbsp finely chopped chives
or parsley

Hash browns with bacon rolls

Plum tomatoes and honeyed bacon roast themselves, while you grate the potatoes and onion, and fry them into sweet-smelling, herb-strewn hash browns.

Heat the oven to 200°C/Gas 6. Cut the tomatoes in half lengthwise, season with sea salt and pepper, and arrange on a baking tray. Roll the bacon rashers into tight rolls and place on the same tray. Drizzle bacon rolls with honey and bake for 20 minutes, or until the tomatoes are soft and the bacon is crisp.

Peel the potatoes and onion, coarsely grate them, then wrap in a clean cloth and squeeze out excess liquid. Place in a bowl, add the beaten egg, flour, chopped herbs, 1 tsp sea salt and the olive oil, and stir well.

Heat 1 tbsp vegetable oil in a fry pan until hot, then add 2 heaped tablespoons of the potato mixture. Squash them flat and fry gently on both sides until golden brown. Keep them warm in the oven while you cook the remaining hash browns, adding a little extra oil to the pan each time.

Serve the hash browns topped with the roasted tomato halves, crisp bacon rolls and rosemary.

SERVES 4

4 plum tomatoes

sea salt

freshly ground black pepper

8 thin rashers rindless bacon,
   halved if large

1 tsp runny honey

6 medium potatoes

1 small onion

1 large free-range egg, beaten

1 tbsp plain flour

2 tbsp chopped herbs
   (eg thyme, rosemary, chives)

1 tbsp olive oil

3 tbsp vegetable oil

rosemary sprigs, to serve

herby Potatoes, crisp honeyed bacon

terry's fried egg

Terry's fried egg roll

My football-mad husband has devised a number of different things to eat while watching sport on television. For this simple half-time lunch, he has even developed a brilliant technique for cooking the perfect fried egg.

Heat the olive oil in a non-stick pan. Break in the eggs, cover the pan with a lid and cook over a very gentle heat for 4 to 5 minutes, depending on the heat, until the whites have set and the yolks have glazed over but are still softly runny.

In the meantime, lightly warm the baguette in the oven for 2 minutes, or split in half and lightly grill the inside surfaces.

Halve the cherry tomatoes. Heat 1 tbsp olive oil in a non-stick fry pan. Add the tomatoes and cook for 2 minutes, until they soften.

Place the split baguettes on two warm plates and lightly butter if you like. Line each one with ham, place a fried egg on top and spoon the cherry tomatoes over. Scatter with salt and pepper and serve.

MAKES 2

Terry's fried eggs:
1 tsp olive oil
2 free-range eggs

To serve:
1 fresh baguette
4 cherry tomatoes
1 tbsp olive oil
butter to spread (optional)
2 thin slices good ham
sea salt
freshly ground black pepper

Chorizo and potatoes

Use mild or spicy chorizo sausages from the deli or butcher, and serve this lovely Spanish tapa dish with crusty bread and a glass of red.

Peel the potatoes and cut into roughly 1 cm dice. Cook in simmering salted water for 10 minutes, until half-cooked.

Slice the chorizo, and finely slice the onion and celery. Heat half the oil in a heavy-based fry pan and sear the chorizo on both sides until browned. Remove the chorizo, then add the remaining oil to the pan and cook the onion and celery for 5 minutes to soften.

Add the potatoes, garlic, sea salt, pepper, and half the paprika; toss well. Add the white wine, bay leaf and enough water to cover the potatoes. Cook, uncovered, over a medium heat for 10 minutes or until the potatoes are tender.

Return the chorizo to the pan and cook on a high heat for a further 5 minutes or until the liquid reduces to a sludgy sauce. Serve warm or at room temperature, scattered with the remaining paprika.

SERVES 4

500 g all-purpose potatoes

salt

2 chorizo sausages

1 onion, peeled

1 celery stick

2 tbsp olive oil

1 garlic clove, smashed

sea salt

freshly ground black pepper

1 tsp paprika

200 ml dry white wine

1 bay leaf

burger with the lot

Burger with the lot

The hamburger is a legitimate and respectable meal of grilled meat and salad served with bread. It's just served vertically, instead of horizontally. The real key to a good burger is in the build, which is both an art and a science.

SERVES 4

Burgers:

2 slices white bread

100 ml milk

500 g prime minced beef

1 tbsp finely snipped chives

1 tbsp finely chopped parsley

sea salt

freshly ground black pepper

1 free-range egg, lightly
    beaten

4 slices bacon or pancetta

1 tbsp olive oil

To serve:

4 slices cheese (eg jarlsberg)

4 hamburger buns

4 tbsp tomato relish (see right)

8 lettuce leaves

2 tomatoes, thickly sliced

2 tbsp quality mayonnaise

To make the burgers, soak the bread in the milk, squeeze dry and chop finely. In a bowl, mix the minced beef with the bread, chives, parsley, salt and pepper. Add the egg, and mix to a mulch with your hands. Form into four thick bun-sized patties, cover and chill.

Grill or pan-fry the bacon or pancetta until crisp. Heat the olive oil in a heavy-based frying pan and cook the burgers for 3 minutes on each side until well browned. Top each with a cheese slice as it comes off the heat.

Split the buns, and lightly toast the insides only. Top the base bun in this order: tomato relish, lettuce leaves, cheese burger, bacon and a slice of tomato. Spread the mayonnaise on the inside lid and place on top.

Tomato relish

Combine 400 g canned chopped tomatoes, 2 tbsp olive oil, 1 finely chopped onion, 2 crushed garlic cloves, 2 tbsp wine vinegar and 1 tbsp sugar in a saucepan. Season and cook down until thick and pulpy, stirring occasionally.

Turkey burger

Go beyond the beef burger to the turkey or chicken burger, which is lighter and sweeter. If you find hamburger buns a bit soft and squishy, try lightly toasted English muffins. These are slightly smaller, so it is easier to shape your burger to them.

In a bowl, combine the minced meat, thyme or parsley, breadcrumbs, egg, and salt and pepper, and mix with your hands to a mulch. Form the mixture into four balls, then flatten into muffin-sized patties.

If grilling, brush the meat with the olive oil. If pan-frying, heat the oil in a heavy-based frying pan. Grill or fry the burgers on both sides until brown and sizzling. This should take around 5 minutes on each side, but check one before serving.

Split the muffins and lightly toast or grill the insides only. Top each muffin base with a lettuce leaf, cucumber slices and the burger, adding tomato and avocado slices if you like. Top with cranberry sauce and mayonnaise, and finally the bun lid.

SERVES 4

Burgers:
450g minced turkey or chicken
1 tbsp thyme leaves or chopped parsley
3 tbsp fresh or dried breadcrumbs
1 free-range egg, lightly beaten
sea salt
freshly ground black pepper
1 tbsp olive oil

To serve:
4 English muffins or hamburger buns
4 soft lettuce leaves
$\frac{1}{2}$ cucumber, peeled and sliced
2 tbsp cranberry sauce
2 tbsp quality mayonnaise

Extras:
2 tomatoes, sliced
$\frac{1}{2}$ avocado, sliced

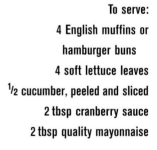

281

chicken stir-fry

Chicken stir-fry

The three rules of the stir-fry are: keep it hot, keep it moving and keep it simple. Flip the food constantly in the wok, and it will stay bright and clear-tasting. It also pays to get everything ready and lined up in order, so nothing is forgotten. (Saves you from that old oops-forgot-to-add-the-chicken syndrome.)

Finely slice the chicken breasts and cut each slice in half. Mix 1 tbsp soy sauce, 1 tbsp rice wine and 1 tsp cornflour together in a bowl. Add the chicken and turn to coat well. Set aside to marinate.

Slice the mangetout lengthwise with the tip of a sharp knife – a bit of an effort but worth it for the effect. Finely slice the celery. Mix the remaining rice wine and cornflour together and set aside.

Heat the wok until hot. When hot, add the oil and stir-fry the garlic and ginger for 30 seconds. Add the chicken with its marinade, and toss well over a high heat for 2 minutes until coloured.

Add the mangetout, celery and bean sprouts, and toss over high heat for 2 minutes. Add the oyster sauce and remaining soy, and toss for 2 minutes. Add the cornflour mixture and bring to the boil, tossing.

Divide the stir-fry between four deep warmed bowls and serve with bowls of rice and chopsticks.

SERVES 4

2 chicken breast fillets

3 tbsp soy sauce

2 tbsp Chinese rice wine or
   dry sherry

2 tsp cornflour

200 g mangetout (snow peas)

2 celery sticks

2 tbsp vegetable oil

1 garlic clove, squashed

1 slice fresh root ginger,
   shredded

200 g bean sprouts, rinsed

2 tbsp oyster sauce

Chinese spiced beef

A simple, old-fashioned cut of meat cooks itself to tenderness in this classic Chinese braise. I serve it with the garlic, ginger and whole spices intact, but you can fish them out if you like.

Cut the beef into 2.5 cm cubes. Heat the oil in a flameproof casserole or heavy-based saucepan and brown the meat lightly, in batches. Return all meat to the pan and add cold water to cover. Bring to the boil, then immediately reduce to a simmer, skimming if necessary.

Stir in the rice wine, garlic, ginger, spring onions, soy sauce, sugar, star anise and cinnamon sticks. Simmer very gently, partly covered, for 2 hours. Meanwhile, soak the mushrooms in the hot water.

Cut the pumpkin into 2 cm cubes, discarding seeds and skin. Drain and halve the mushrooms, discarding stalks.

Add the pumpkin and mushrooms to the braise and cook uncovered, for another 30 minutes until the beef is tender. Serve in warm bowls, with lots of rice.

SERVES 4

1 kg beef brisket

2 tbsp vegetable oil

3 tbsp Chinese rice wine or dry sherry

2 garlic cloves, bruised

3 thick slices fresh root ginger

3 spring onions, finely chopped

125 ml soy sauce

3 tbsp soft brown sugar

4 star anise

4 cinnamon sticks

8 dried Chinese mushrooms

200 ml hot water

500 g pumpkin or butternut squash

spices

toast before use

There is nothing wrong with buying ground or powdered spices, but you will get more flavour if you buy whole spices and lightly toast them in a dry fry pan as you need them. Grind in an electric coffee grinder or pulverise with a pestle and mortar.

cinnamon coconut rice

Place 300g rinsed jasmine rice in a pan with 300ml coconut milk, 300ml water, salt, 2 cinnamon sticks and 2 star anise, and bring to the boil. Cover tightly and simmer very gently, undisturbed, for 15 minutes. Rest for 10 minutes, then fluff up with a fork and serve with curry.

cinnamon toast

Shake 2 tbsp granulated sugar with 1–2 tsp ground cinnamon in a jar. Grill the bread on one side, turn, butter the untoasted side, sprinkle with cinnamon sugar and lightly grill until melted.

sticky cardamom toffee syrup

Gently heat 150g soft brown sugar, 25ml cream, 1 split vanilla pod, 2 tbsp butter and 2 crushed cardamom pods until the sugar dissolves, then simmer for 5 minutes. Strain and serve over steamed puds, cakes and poached pears.

sweet, mulled wine

Combine 750ml light red wine and 250ml Muscat or port with a split vanilla pod, 2 cinnamon sticks, 8 cloves, 2 bay leaves and the rind of half an orange. Cover and leave overnight to infuse. Heat gently, add 200g sugar, stirring, and serve warm.

clever with cloves

Strong little spikes of punchy flavour, cloves are the dried flower buds of an evergreen tree native to Indonesia. Stick them in an onion when cooking savoury dishes, or an orange for sweet dishes, so you can take them out easily at the end.

grind your own nutmeg

Whole nutmeg is far superior to ready ground. Freshly grate or grind for cakes, soups, custards, quiches and rice pud.

the joy of red-cooking

Make a brilliant Chinese braise with 250 ml soy sauce, 200 ml chicken stock, 2 tbsp rice wine or dry sherry, 1 tsp sesame oil, some fresh ginger and garlic, 1 tbsp sugar and 3 star anise, and simmer for 10 minutes. Use it to poach Chinese mushrooms, chicken, fish or pork, to serve with rice.

dip into Egyptian dukkah

In a hot, dry pan, toast 100 g sesame seeds, 100 g blanched almonds, 50 g coriander seeds and 10 g cumin seeds until fragrant, stirring. Cool, then coarsely grind with 1 tsp sea salt and ½ tsp pepper. Serve with warm Turkish bread and olive oil.

a great rice pulao

Fry 1 chopped onion in 1 tbsp oil. Add 1 tsp each cumin seeds and brown mustard seeds, 2 crushed cardamom pods, 1 bay leaf, 1 cinnamon stick, salt, pepper and ½ tsp each of ground cumin, coriander and turmeric. Add 300 g rinsed rice and 600 ml boiling water, cover and simmer very gently for 15 minutes.

Sweet cinnamon, bitter saffron, nutty coriander, and floral nutmeg teach us to cook with all of our senses, adding warmth and perfume by the spoonful.

Cavatappi with sausage

Cavatappi is my pasta of the moment, because its corkscrew curls catch and keep all the sauce. And this is my favourite sauce – spicy Italian pork sausage cooked in milk (a grand-motherly trick to make it sweet), and then in tomato. You can't get more comforting than that.

Slit open the sausages and remove the meat, discarding the skins. Finely slice the onion. Heat the olive oil and butter in a fry pan and cook the onion gently for 5 or 6 minutes until soft but not coloured.

Pinch the meat into the pan and fry, breaking it up with a wooden spoon, until it is cooked but not browned. Add the milk and simmer very gently, stirring, for 5 minutes until it is all absorbed.

Roughly chop the tomatoes and add them, with their juices, to the pan. Add the sugar, nutmeg, and salt and pepper, and simmer for 15 minutes, stirring occasionally.

In the meantime, cook the pasta in a large pot of boiling salted water until al dente, tender but still firm to the bite.

Add the cream to the sauce and stir, gently heating it through. Drain the pasta, toss well with the sauce and serve with plenty of grated parmesan.

SERVES 4

6 small, spicy Italian pork sausages, or 3 large ones

1 small onion, peeled

1 tbsp olive oil

1 tbsp butter

150 ml milk

400 g canned tomatoes

1 tsp sugar

pinch of freshly grated nutmeg

sea salt

freshly ground black pepper

400 g cavatappi, penne or other short tube pasta

2 tbsp cream (optional)

freshly grated parmesan

Penne with tuna

Cook little cubes of potato in the same pot as the pasta, and they'll be soft and lush by the time they hit the tuna and caper sauce. If you need an extra flavour hit, add a finely chopped red chilli with the olives.

Peel the potatoes and chop into 1 cm cubes. Bring a large pot of salted water to the boil, add the pasta and potatoes and cook together until tender, around 10 minutes depending on the pasta.

Drain the tuna, reserving the oil. Heat the olive oil in a pan, and add the tuna, olives and capers. Toss well until everything is hot.

Drain the cooked pasta and potatoes and add to the sauce with most of the tuna oil. Add the basil or rocket leaves with sea salt and pepper, and toss well over the heat until wilted.

SERVES 4

4 medium potatoes

500g penne or rigatoni

300g canned tuna in olive oil

1 tbsp olive oil

20 small black olives

2 tbsp salted capers, rinsed

small bunch of basil, or 100g
 baby rocket leaves

sea salt

freshly ground black pepper

Orecchiette with rocket

Finely slice 2 red chillies and 2 garlic cloves. Gently heat with 2 tbsp extra virgin olive oil in a big fry pan, stirring. Add 300g rocket leaves and toss until wilted, then add 450g cooked, drained orecchiette or similar pasta. Toss well and scatter with grated parmesan.

Baked spaghetti

The good thing about this supper is that you can cook everything beforehand and put it together, then just bake in the oven when you're ready to eat.

Finely chop the onion. Heat the olive oil in a large fry pan and cook the onion for 10 minutes. Add the garlic and minced meat and stir over high heat until it browns. Sprinkle with flour and cook, stirring, for 3 minutes.

Add the white wine and boil for 1 minute, then add the tomatoes, tomato purée, stock, sea salt, pepper, nutmeg and rosemary sprigs. Partially cover and cook gently for 45 minutes.

Heat the oven to 180°C/Gas 4. Cook the pasta in plenty of boiling salted water until tender but firm. Drain well, then toss with the sauce. Scatter with parmesan, pile into a lightly oiled serving dish and bake for 30 minutes until crisp on top.

SERVES 4

1 onion, peeled
2 tbsp olive oil
2 garlic cloves, peeled
and crushed
500g minced pork,
veal or beef
1 tbsp plain flour
125ml white wine
800g canned chopped
tomatoes
1 tbsp tomato purée (paste)
250ml chicken stock or water
sea salt
freshly ground black pepper
½ tsp freshly grated nutmeg
few rosemary or oregano sprigs
500g spaghetti
2 tbsp freshly grated parmesan

Beans and wilted rocket

I suspect I spend more on peppery, horseradishy rocket than I do on shoes. I wilt it into pasta, scatter it over risotto and stews, serve it with seafood grills, and generally munch my way through bowls of the stuff. This is a fast (rocket-fuelled) way to get lunch on the table.

Heat 2 tbsp olive oil in a saucepan. Add the garlic, tomatoes or passata, sugar, Worcestershire sauce and mustard, and cook gently for 10 minutes, stirring. Add the beans and parsley, and cook for a further 5 minutes, adding a little water if it gets too thick. Season with salt and pepper to taste.

Drop the rocket into a pot of simmering salted water for a few seconds until just wilted, then drain well, squeeze out excess water, and chop roughly. Toss in 1 tbsp olive oil, with sea salt and pepper.

Grill or toast four thick slices of sourdough bread. Top each slice with the wilted rocket, and spoon the hot beans over the top.

SERVES 6

3 tbsp extra virgin olive oil

2 garlic cloves, crushed

400 g canned tomatoes, chopped
   or 500 ml tomato passata
   (puréed tomatoes)

1 tbsp soft brown sugar

1 tbsp Worcestershire sauce

1 tsp Dijon mustard

800 g canned white beans
   (cannellini or white kidney
   beans), drained and rinsed

2 tbsp finely chopped parsley

sea salt

freshly ground black pepper

250 g rocket leaves

4 thick slices sourdough bread

Stuffed peppers

It's time some of these old-fashioned ideas were brought back into circulation, because they work. Stuff a sweet pepper with meat and rice, and the juices will mingle as the stuffing virtually steams and the pepper cooks, so that the two are one.

Heat the oven to 200°C / Gas 6. Cut the tops off the peppers, retaining them to use as lids. Scoop out the seeds and cut away any major internal ribbing from the insides.

In a bowl, mix the minced meat with the egg, cooked rice, spring onions, half the paprika, parsley, sea salt and pepper, mulching it with your hands. Add half the tomatoes, mixing well.

Stuff the peppers with the mixture, piling it high. Stand the peppers in a lightly oiled baking tin and rub the skin with a little of the olive oil. Bake for 1 hour, or until tender, adding the lightly oiled pepper lids to the tin for the last 15 minutes.

To make the sauce, gently heat the rest of the chopped tomatoes with the remaining olive oil, paprika, sugar, salt and pepper.

To serve, place a whole stuffed pepper on each plate, spoon the tomato sauce on and around, and top with the lid.

SERVES 4

2 sweet red peppers
2 sweet yellow peppers
500g minced pork or chicken
1 free-range egg
150g cooked rice
4 spring onions, finely chopped
1 tsp paprika
1 tbsp finely chopped parsley
sea salt
freshly ground black pepper
400g canned chopped tomatoes
2 tbsp olive oil
1 tsp sugar

sweets
& treats

Cranberry jelly and cream

This sparkling dessert jelly is made with easily obtainable cranberry juice. Add a splosh of port for those old enough to remember port wine jelly.

In a saucepan, combine the cranberry juice, sugar, and port if using. Heat slowly to just under the boil, stirring to dissolve the sugar. Remove the pan from the heat.

Soak the leaf gelatine in cold water for 3 minutes until blobby, then squeeze out the excess water and whisk the gelatine into the hot cranberry liquid until melted. Or sprinkle the powdered gelatine directly over the hot liquid and leave for 1 minute, then whisk well.

SERVES 4

700 ml cranberry juice

100 g sugar

50 ml ruby port (optional)

4 sheets of leaf gelatine or
    22 g powdered gelatine

100 ml single cream

Leave to cool, stirring occasionally. When cool, pour the cranberry liquid into four 150 ml dry martini glasses or jelly moulds and chill in the refrigerator until set.

If set in glasses, trickle a little cream over the top of each jelly until you have a smooth cream 'frosting', then serve. If set in moulds, turn out onto plates and drizzle with the cream.

Berry mascarpone

My lighter, summery version of tiramisu uses strawberries, raspberries and berry liqueur instead of coffee and cocoa. Like a traditional tiramisu, it goes all cakey, spongey and creamy, as the flavours swell and ripen.

Halve or quarter the strawberries lengthwise and set aside with the raspberries. In a bowl, beat the eggs and sugar together until creamy, then whisk in the mascarpone until smooth.

Mix the liqueur and milk in a shallow bowl. One at a time, dip half the sponge fingers in the liquid, just long enough to coat, and arrange over the base of a large, but not too deep, serving dish.

Cover with a layer of mascarpone cream and scatter with berries. Repeat with another layer of dipped sponge fingers, then mascarpone. Top with a generous layer of berries, allowing some to sink into the cream. Chill for 4 or 5 hours before serving.

Note: this recipe contains raw egg.

SERVES 6

500 g strawberries, hulled
250 g raspberries
3 large free-range eggs
100 g caster sugar
500 g mascarpone
100 ml pink berry liqueur
(eg Framboise)
100 ml milk
200 g Italian sponge fingers
(savoiardi)

lemon posset

Lemon posset

In medieval England, a posset was a sweetened, lightly curdled milk drink. The modern posset is of cream and sugar, acidulated with lemon juice. It's just like a rich, gooey lemon curd without all that mucking around with egg yolks.

Combine the cream and caster sugar in a saucepan and bring to the boil, stirring. Reduce the heat and bubble for 3 minutes, stirring constantly, without allowing the cream to boil over.

Remove from the heat and add the lemon juice, stirring well. Taste, and add a little more lemon juice if you so desire. Leave the posset to cool for 10 minutes, then stir once more and pour into four 100 ml ramekins, Chinese tea cups or espresso coffee cups.

Cool the posset and chill in the refrigerator for a few hours before serving, with tiny spoons.

SERVES 4

450 ml double or whipping
   cream

125 g caster sugar

60 ml lemon juice

Pineapple vodka crush

This is so spritzy and refreshing that people put a spoonful in their mouth and immediately go 'wow'. It's great at the end of a barbecue, or after something spicy. And if you put it in the freezer and forget to stir it, don't worry, the vodka prevents it from freezing into a solid block – after 15 minutes in the fridge it will be soft enough to serve.

Cut the top off the pineapple and slice lengthwise into quarters. Slice off and discard the core, then cut the skin and the 'eyes' away from the flesh. Cut the pineapple flesh into cubes.

Whiz the pineapple flesh in a blender with the vodka, sugar, lemon juice and mint leaves.

Pour the mixture into a plastic container or ice-cream tray and freeze for an hour or two until firm on the outside and still liquid in the centre. Tip the mixture into a bowl and beat well, then return to the freezer for another hour or so, until partly frozen. Beat again, breaking up any crystals, then freeze until required.

Chill 4 bowls or glasses, and leave the pineapple crush in the refrigerator for 15 minutes to soften before serving. Scoop into the chilled bowls or glasses and serve, with a sprig of mint on the side.

SERVES 4

1 kg pineapple

100 ml vodka

100 g caster sugar

1 tbsp lemon juice

15 mint leaves

4 mint sprigs

Chocolate bourbon balls

If you've ever made chocolate truffles, you will know they can be quite tricky. These aren't, but they are just as delicious. And if you're feeling flash, decorate with edible gold leaf, available from cake decoration shops.

Finely chop the chocolate. Heat the cream in a saucepan, stirring until it bubbles, then remove from the heat, add the chocolate and stir until melted.

Whiz the sponge fingers in a food processor, or crush with a rolling pin to fine crumbs.

MAKES 50

160g dark, bitter chocolate

125ml whipping cream

250g Italian sponge fingers (savoiardi)

100g icing sugar

3 tbsp cocoa powder

100g ground almonds

100g finely chopped walnuts

3 tbsp bourbon, or whisky

180g butter, melted

cocoa powder for dusting

Sift the icing sugar and cocoa powder into a large bowl. Mix in the crumbs, ground almonds and chopped walnuts. Add the bourbon, chocolate cream and butter and mix well.

Take a walnut-sized pinch of the mixture and roll into a ball in your hands. (If too wet, add a little more cocoa powder. If a little dry, add a dash more bourbon.) Place on greaseproof paper on a tray, and refrigerate for at least 4 hours until firm. Roll each chocolate bourbon ball in cocoa powder to serve.

Frozen chocolate mousse

This is better than ice-cream: a rich, creamy, gooey, moussey parfait, ready to slice, chop or scoop. Use a light hand to fold the cream into the chocolate mixture: better to have a few streaks of cream through the mousse than lose all the lightness and volume.

Melt the chocolate in a heatproof bowl set over a pan of gently simmering water, then set aside to cool for 3 minutes.

In a bowl, beat the eggs, egg yolks and sugar together for a few minutes, using a hand-held electric beater, until pale and thick. Add the melted chocolate and beat constantly for about 3 minutes, then stir in the vanilla extract and whisky.

In another bowl, beat the cream until it forms light peaks. Fold the cream lightly through the chocolate, then pour into a 1 litre loaf tin. Cover with cling film and freeze overnight.

To serve, soften the mousse in the refrigerator for 15 minutes, or dip the base of the tin very briefly in hot water and run a knife around the edges. Turn out and cut into thick slices or chunks, or scoop straight from the tin. Serve immediately, dusted with cocoa powder.

Note: this recipe contains raw egg.

SERVES 6

200g dark, bittersweet
    chocolate, chopped

2 large free-range eggs, plus
    2 egg yolks

100g caster sugar

1 tsp vanilla extract

2 tbsp whisky, Cognac or
    Amaretto liqueur

250ml whipping cream

bitter cocoa powder to dust

Banana ice-cream

All the fun of banana ice-cream, without the sugar, eggs or cream. Peel 8 firm ripe bananas, wrap in cling film and freeze overnight. Soften for 20 minutes, then roughly chop and whiz until thick and creamy. Eat now, or refreeze, in which case soften for 20 minutes before you slice or scoop.

Baked banana split

Bake 4 unpeeled bananas at 180°C/Gas 4
for 30 minutes until the skin is black. Finely chop
100 g dark, bitter chocolate and 2 tbsp walnuts. Gently slit
the skin and peel back the top part. Scatter the split with
chocolate and nuts, then serve with ice-cream.

Espresso prunes

Dissolve 2 tbsp ground espresso coffee in 125 ml boiling water, then strain. Add 300 g sugar, 2 tbsp brandy and 500 ml water and bring to the boil, stirring. Add 500 g large dried, pitted prunes and gently simmer for 30 minutes until the liquid is thick and syrupy. Serve with yoghurt.

Simple passionfruit soufflé

Even the biggest scaredy cat can now make a soufflé. This is based on the lightest, tangiest, most beautiful soufflé in the world, that of the revered (and retired) Fredy Girardet of Switzerland. There are no sauces to make and no sorcery to employ – just egg yolks and whites, passionfruit and sugar.

Heat the oven to 200°C/Gas 6. Butter the insides of four small individual soufflé dishes or ramekins, lightly dust each one with 1 tsp sugar, tipping out any excess, and place on a baking tray.

Strain the passionfruit pulp until you have 50 ml juice; discard the seeds. In a bowl, beat the egg yolks with 60 g caster sugar until pale and smooth. Add the passionfruit juice, beating well.

Whisk the 5 egg whites in a large, clean bowl. Add 20 g sugar and whisk until they start to thicken. Add the remaining sugar and keep whisking until soft peaks form. Gently fold one third of the egg whites into the yolks, then fold in the remainder.

Fill the soufflé dishes to the brim and smooth the tops. Bake just below the middle of the oven for 10 minutes until puffed and golden.

Dust each soufflé with icing sugar, gently place on a serving plate and serve immediately, with cream or ice-cream to one side.

SERVES 4
1 tbsp melted butter
100 g caster sugar, plus 4 tsp
100 ml passionfruit pulp
    (about 4 passionfruit)
3 free-range eggs, separated,
    plus 2 extra egg whites
icing sugar to dust

Lemon sugar crêpes

When I was a child, Italian restaurants served a magical dish of hot golden crêpes with lemon juice and sugar. Use granulated sugar for a crunch to contrast with the velvety smooth crêpes.

Blend the flour, sugar, salt, melted butter, whole egg and egg yolk in the food processor. Add the milk gradually, with the motor running, to make a smooth and creamy batter. Rest for at least 30 minutes.

Brush a crêpe pan or small non-stick frying pan with melted butter and place over a medium heat. When hot, add a ladleful of batter and swirl the pan so it covers the base thinly. Cook for a minute or two until the base is lightly golden.

Turn the crêpe over and cook the other side very briefly. Slide onto a warm plate, sprinkle with sugar, and roll into a tight cigar-like cylinder. Cover and keep warm while you do the rest.

Serve two crepês per person on warm plates, sprinkled with extra sugar and lemon juice. Serve with ice-cream and a wedge of lemon.

MAKES 8
Batter:
100g plain flour
40g caster sugar
pinch of salt
1 tbsp melted butter
1 free-range egg, plus
1 egg yolk
200ml milk
extra melted butter to cook

To serve:
2 tbsp granulated sugar
juice of 2 lemons
1 lemon, quartered

Moroccan rice pud

A creamy, plump rice pudding, scented with cinnamon and fragrant orange flower water – cooked in the pot.

Combine the rice, salt, milk, water and cinnamon stick in a heavy-based saucepan and bring to the boil, stirring constantly to prevent the rice sticking.

Reduce the heat and simmer at a gentle bubble, stirring from time to time, for 15 to 20 minutes or until the rice is plump, but the texture is still slightly runny.

Remove the cinnamon stick. Add the butter, sugar and orange flower water, and stir until dissolved.

Spoon the rice into warmed pudding bowls and serve warm or at room temperature, dusted with cinnamon.

SERVES 4
180g arborio (risotto) rice
pinch of salt
600ml milk
150ml water
1 cinnamon stick
1 tsp butter
3 tbsp caster sugar
2 tbsp orange flower water, or rosewater
1 tsp ground cinnamon or nutmeg for dusting

Gooey chocolate pud

An oozy, boozy chocolate pudding with a soft, gooey – almost liquid – centre.

Heat the oven to 190°C/Gas 5. Butter four 150ml heatproof soufflé dishes or ramekins and place on a baking tray. Chop the chocolate roughly and melt in a heatproof bowl set over a pot of gently simmering water. Remove from the heat, stir well and allow to cool slightly.

Beat in the vanilla essence, brandy and sugar. Beat in the egg yolks, one by one, and then the flour. The mixture will be fairly stiff.

Whisk or beat the egg whites until stiff and peaky, then gently fold them into the chocolate mixture. Pour into the dishes and bake for 10 to 12 minutes until puffed and well risen. The puddings should still be gooey inside.

SERVES 4

1 tsp butter

150g dark, bitter chocolate

½ tsp vanilla essence

1 tbsp brandy, rum or whisky

85g caster sugar

4 large free-range eggs,
    separated

1 tbsp plain flour, sifted

fruit

Warm spiced cherries Make a syrup by heating 100g sugar with 200ml water, a squeeze of lemon juice and 4 cloves. Add 300g pitted ripe cherries and gently poach for 2 minutes. Add 2 tbsp cherry or berry liqueur and serve warm with thick cream or a wedge of chocolate cake.

Spicy saffron pears Peel 4 ripe, firm pears and poach in a syrup made by heating 100g sugar with a good pinch of saffron, a few cardamom pods and enough dry white wine to cover. Serve with a dollop of yoghurt and a grind of black pepper.

Caramel apples Peel, quarter and core 4 apples and sizzle in a non-stick fry pan with 2 tbsp butter, 2 tbsp soft brown sugar and 2 tbsp sultanas until golden. Serve with ice-cream or crème fraîche.

Peach and prosciutto Serve a perfect fresh peach with a platter of thinly sliced prosciutto, a wedge of lemon and a generous rocket and parmesan salad for a summer lunch. Or cut the peach into segments and wrap in a short length of prosciutto for nibbles with drinks.

Vineyard sausages Slowly sizzle some well-pricked garlicky pork sausages in a pan, then add a handful of green grapes. Cook until the grapes warm, split, and spill their juices into the pan. Serve the sausages on a rocket salad with the grapey juices spooned over.

Red berry wine Press a punnet of fresh berries through a fine sieve, and stir the juices into 4 glasses of well chilled dessert wine. Add a dash of Cointreau or berry liqueur to sweeten if it tastes too tart.

Red berry meringues Crush two thirds of a punnet of raspberries with a fork, then gently mix with the remaining whole berries. Sandwich 16 crisp little meringues together with 150ml whipped cream and the berries for a dessert or afternoon tea.

Toffee lime bananas Cut 4 unpeeled bananas in half lengthwise. Sprinkle the cut sides with 4 tsp granulated sugar and place under the grill until the sugar bubbles and browns. Serve the soft bananas with chilled crème fraîche, soured cream or ice-cream and a lime wedge.

Balsamic strawberries Wash 450g strawberries and hull. Place in a bowl with 2 tbsp balsamic vinegar and a grind of black pepper, toss lightly and leave for an hour before serving. The vinegar and pepper intensify the flavour and tend to disappear into the berries.

Berry swizzlers Thread blueberries, strawberries and raspberries on little bamboo skewers. Dust with icing sugar and serve as a chic dessert with yoghurt for dipping – or use as a swizzle stick in cocktails, fruit punches and fresh fruit smoothies.

Frosted grapes A pretty way to finish a cake, fruit tart or jelly. Frost little bunches of 3 or 4 grapes, by painting the grapes with lightly whisked egg white and gently rolling them in caster sugar.

Sunday roast fruit When next you roast a leg of pork or duckling, cut 4 mandarins or clementines in half and add them to the roasting juices for the last 30 minutes. Serve warm, ready to squeeze over the meat for an instant citrus sauce.

red berry meringues

chocolate pear pudding

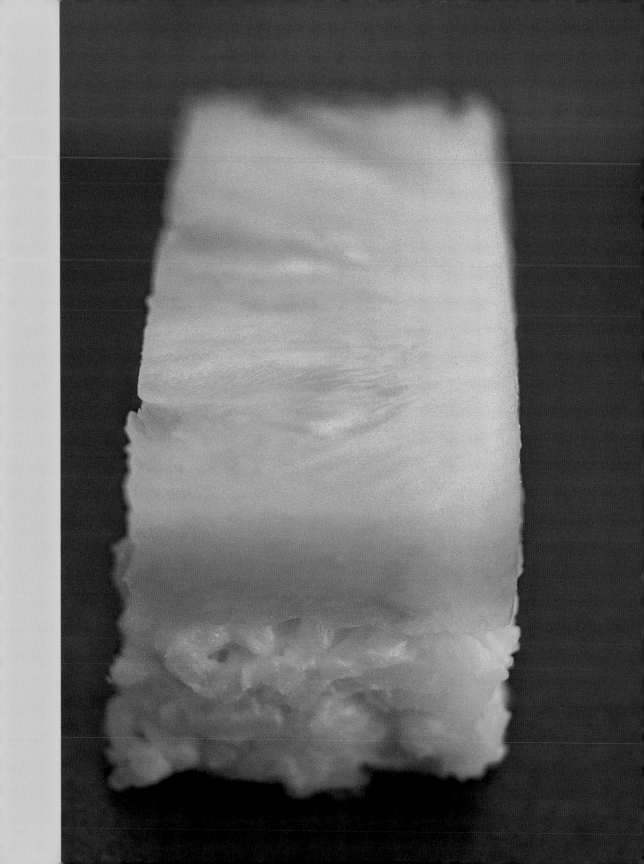

Chocolate pear pudding

I like these two-for-the-price-of-one puds. In this lush, gooey chocolate pud, you also get tender baked pears peeking out. If your pears are slightly under-ripe, first poach them in white wine and sugar for 10 minutes.

Heat the oven to 170°C / Gas 3. Beat the butter and sugar together in a bowl until smooth. Add the eggs, one at a time, beating well.

Sift the flour, cocoa powder and baking powder together over the mixture and beat well with a wooden spoon. Add the milk, stirring until smooth. Spoon the mixture into a lightly buttered 30 x 20 cm pie dish or gratin dish and spread evenly.

Peel the pears and cut a 1 cm slice from the base of each one so they will stand upright. Push them firmly into the mixture.

Bake for 30 minutes or until the pudding has puffed up around the pears and set at the edges, but is still a bit gooey in the centre. Serve with cream or crème fraîche.

SERVES 4

125g butter, melted

200g caster sugar

3 large free-range eggs

180g plain flour

75g cocoa powder

1 tsp baking powder

70ml milk

4 ripe pears (eg Conference)

Pineapple sushi

No, not sushi as in raw fish, but sushi as in sweet coconut rice topped with fresh tangy pineapple. Fresh mango works beautifully, too. You can pick the sushi up and eat them in your fingers, or serve with a dessert knife and fork.

Put the rice, sugar, coconut milk and water in a saucepan, and bring to the boil, stirring constantly to prevent sticking. Simmer very gently, uncovered, on the lowest possible heat for 20 minutes; stir occasionally, and keep an eye on it to avoid any boiling over.

Once the rice has absorbed the liquid but is not yet cooked, cover the pan tightly and leave over the same gentle heat for another 10 minutes until the rice is tender.

Lightly rinse out a 20 x 15 cm shallow tin or pie dish. Tip in the rice and spread it out evenly, to a 2 cm depth. Smooth the top and leave to cool. Cover with cling film and chill for an hour or two.

When chilled, cut the rice into fingers, about 3 x 8 cm. Trim the pineapple flesh into matching oblongs, and place on top. Serve one or two sushi fingers per person.

MAKES 12

300 g sushi rice

100 g caster sugar

200 ml canned coconut milk

400 ml water

500 g peeled, cored fresh pineapple

Little lemon pots

Tangy little lemon custards can be baked ahead and served at room temperature, making them perfect for entertaining. You'll need 2 to 3 lemons, depending on their size. Serve with the coconut macaroons on page 350, for crunch.

Heat the oven to 160°C/Gas 3. Whisk the eggs and sugar in a bowl until well mixed. Stir in the lemon rind and juice, and lightly whisk in the cream.

Skim off and discard any froth, then strain the custard into six 100 ml ovenproof pots or Chinese ovenproof white tea cups.

Stand in a shallow baking tin, and fill the tin with hot water to come halfway up the sides of the pots. Bake for 20 to 25 minutes or until the custards have set, with just a tiny wobble on the surface. Remove from the baking tin.

Serve either warm or at room temperature, dusted with icing sugar.

SERVES 6

6 large free-range eggs

175g caster sugar

2 tsp grated lemon rind

125ml lemon juice

150ml single or whipping
   cream

icing sugar for dusting

blood orange jelly

Blood orange jelly

As wobbly as a runaway bride, this do-ahead jelly fills the mouth with its powerful tang. You'll need 3 to 4 blood oranges, depending on their size.

Put a few spoonfuls of the measured water in a small heatproof bowl and sprinkle with the powdered gelatine. Leave to soften for 5 minutes, then warm gently over a pan of hot water for about 5 minutes until dissolved.

Dissolve the sugar in the remaining water in a small pan, stirring, then bring to the boil. Remove from heat, add the blood orange juice and whisk in the dissolved gelatine.

SERVES 4

200 ml water

15 g powdered gelatine

200 g sugar

250 ml blood orange juice

To serve:

4 slices blood orange

2 tbsp blood orange juice

Rinse four 100 ml moulds with cold water, and shake dry. Fill with the orange liquid, allow to cool, then refrigerate for several hours until set.

To serve, dip the base of each mould very briefly in hot water, run a knife around the edge to loosen the jelly and turn out onto a serving plate. Top each jelly with an orange slice and drizzle with a little extra juice to serve.

Roast vanilla peaches

One of the great quandaries of summer is whether to just scoff all the glorious fruit as it comes to hand, or whether to cook it. Here's one good, very simple and deliciously fragrant reason to cook it.

Heat the oven to 200°C/Gas 6. Combine the white wine, sugar, cinnamon sticks and vanilla pod in a small saucepan. Heat, stirring, until the sugar dissolves, then boil for 1 minute.

Place the peaches in a small, shallow baking tin and pour in the wine mixture. Bake in the centre of the oven for 30 to 40 minutes or until the skins start to split, and the peaches look all toasty and flushed. Strain the juices into a jug.

Serve the peaches warm or at room temperature, drizzled with their cooking juices. If you have any summer berries around, warm them gently in the poaching liquid and serve with the peaches.

SERVES 4 OR 8
750 ml dry white wine
200 g caster sugar
2 cinnamon sticks
1 vanilla pod, split lengthwise
8 firm, ripe peaches
handful of summer berries
(optional)

Little peach tarts

I don't believe these need either cream or ice-cream, but feel free to disagree.

Heat the oven to 200°C/Gas 6. To peel the peaches, dunk them in a pot of boiling water for 5 seconds and the skins will peel off easily. Halve each peach, cutting around the side of the stone.

Roll out the pastry on a lightly floured surface and cut out eight circles, 10 cm in diameter. Place on lightly oiled baking sheets and brush with beaten egg.

Place a peach half, cut-side down, on top of each pastry round. Drizzle the peaches with a little honey, and dot with butter. Bake for around 20 minutes until the peaches are soft and the pastry is risen and lightly scorched.

Using a warm spoon, drizzle a little more honey over each peach – this will glaze it beautifully. Serve warm or at room temperature.

SERVES 4 OR 8

4 large firm, ripe peaches

500 g packet ready-rolled puff pastry

1 egg, beaten

2 tbsp runny honey

1 tbsp butter, softened

1 extra tbsp runny honey, to serve

Banana bread

This cake-like banana bread will stay moist for several days of breakfasts, brunches, afternoon teas, and I'll-just-have-a-small-slice-before-bed moments.

Heat the oven to 180°C/Gas 4. Lightly butter a 25 x 10cm loaf tin. Sift the flour, baking powder and salt into a bowl; set aside. Mash the bananas to a purée.

Cream the butter and sugar together in a bowl, with a hand-held electric beater, until smooth and pale. Add the eggs one at a time, beating well until just combined.

Fold in the mashed bananas, vanilla and walnuts, using a spatula, then lightly fold in the flour. Spoon the mixture into the loaf tin.

Bake for 1 hour or until a skewer inserted in the middle comes out dry, covering the top with foil if it starts to brown too quickly. Allow to cool in the tin for 20 minutes before turning out. Serve warm or at room temperature, cut into thick slices.

SERVES 6

250g plain flour

2 tsp baking powder

pinch of salt

3 ripe bananas, around 450g

125g butter, softened

150g caster sugar

2 large free-range eggs

½ tsp vanilla extract

50g walnuts, chopped

Rhubarb sponge pud

The good thing about this pudding is that the rhubarb cooks itself under the golden sponge topping.

Heat the oven to 180°C/Gas 4. Cream the butter and sugar together in a bowl until light. Add the eggs, one at a time, beating well. Sift the flour into the bowl, folding it through quickly with a large metal spoon or spatula.

Cut the rhubarb stalks into 2 cm lengths, discarding any leaves. Arrange in a tumbled fashion in a buttered 1 litre pie or baking dish and scatter with the 80 g caster sugar.

Spoon the mixture on top of the fruit and bake for 50 to 60 minutes until the topping is a golden sponge cake and the rhubarb is tender. (If the topping appears to brown too quickly in the oven, cover lightly with foil.) Serve with rich cream.

SERVES 4

Sponge topping:

100 g butter, soft

100 g caster sugar

2 large free-range eggs

100 g self-raising flour, sifted

Fruit filling:

500 g ripe rhubarb stalks

80 g caster sugar

Sugar plums
Brush 8 ripe
plums with beaten
egg white, then roll
in 3 tbsp white sugar to
coat well. Bake on a foil-lined tray
at 200°C/Gas 6 for 15 minutes until
soft. Serve with mascarpone,
or the caramel yoghurt on
page 359.

Little berry cakes

To do these as chic little petits fours, you will need a 24-hole mini-muffin or petit four tray. Otherwise, call them not-so-little berry cakes and bake them in a standard 12-hole muffin tray.

Heat the oven to 170°C/Gas 3. Lightly butter a tray of 12 muffin moulds or 24 mini moulds or line with the appropriate paper cases.

Using an electric mixer, beat the softened butter and sugar together until smooth. Beat in the eggs, one at a time. Sift in the flour and salt, and fold through until well mixed. Finally, stir in the milk and vanilla until smooth.

Spoon the batter into the moulds. Drop a single berry on top of each little cake; place three on muffin-sized cakes.

Bake little cakes for 12 to 15 minutes, larger ones for 18 to 20 minutes, or until a skewer inserted in the centre comes out clean.

Cool to room temperature, dust with icing sugar and serve.

MAKES 12 OR 24
125g butter, softened
125g caster sugar
3 large free-range eggs
180g self-raising flour
pinch of salt
60ml milk
$\frac{1}{2}$ tsp vanilla extract
24–36 raspberries or
blueberries
icing sugar to dust

Coconut macaroons

You can't get much simpler than this: three little ingredients turned into crisp little coconut biscuits to serve with coffee, poached fruits, or the little lemon pots on page 334.

Heat the oven to 180°C/Gas 4. Whisk the egg whites, sugar and coconut together in a bowl until they lightly come together. With wet hands, press the mixture into a flat, square shape about 1 cm high, on a board.

Cut out twelve 4 or 5 cm rounds, using a small pastry cutter or upturned liqueur glass, and place on a lightly oiled or non-stick baking tray.

MAKES 12

2 egg whites

100 g caster sugar

160 g desiccated coconut

Bake in the centre of the oven for 15 minutes until very lightly golden, just touched with colour. Transfer the macaroons to a wire tray to cool. Store in an airtight container for up to 1 week.

just egg white, sugar and coconut

Chocolate cup cakes

Cakes made with cocoa powder are lighter than those made with chocolate. I take this to mean you can eat more of them.

Heat the oven to 180°C/Gas 4. Arrange 12 paper muffin or cup cake cases in a muffin tray.

Using an electric mixer, beat the softened butter and sugar together until smooth. Beat in the eggs, one at a time. Sift in the flour and cocoa powder, and fold through the mixture until well mixed.

Spoon the mixture into the cases and bake for 15 to 20 minutes until the tops spring back to the touch. Leave in the muffin tray for 5 minutes, then transfer to a wire rack to cool completely.

Dust the cup cakes with icing sugar. Or to make the icing, melt the chocolate and butter in a heatproof bowl over simmering water, stir until smooth, then cool for 5 to 10 minutes to thicken. Spread each cup cake with icing, and sprinkle with gold leaf. Leave to set.

MAKES 12
150 g butter, softened
200 g caster sugar
4 large free-range eggs
150 g self-raising flour
50 g bitter cocoa powder
icing sugar to dust

Chocolate icing:
50 g dark, bitter chocolate, chopped
50 g butter
edible gold leaf sprinkles (from cake decorating specialists)

Baby fruit cakes

These soft, fruity little cakes are so easy to make, it's almost spooky. Don't go on a picnic without them.

Heat the oven to 180°C/Gas 4. Combine the butter, sultanas, currants, sugar, mixed spice, cinnamon, ginger, bicarbonate of soda and water in a saucepan. Bring to the boil, stirring, then remove from the heat and allow to cool.

Add the eggs and beat well. Sift the two flours together, add to the mixture, and beat thoroughly.

Pour into lightly buttered or oiled muffin tin moulds or a muffin tray lined with muffin paper cases. Bake for 30 minutes, or until a skewer inserted into the centre comes out clean.

Allow to cool before removing from the moulds. Store in an airtight container for up to 3 days.

MAKES 16

150g butter

300g sultanas

300g currants

180g soft brown sugar

1 tsp ground mixed spice

1 tsp ground cinnamon

1 tsp ground ginger

1 tsp bicarbonate of soda

250ml water

2 eggs, well beaten

150g plain flour

150g self-raising flour

Little chocolate cakes

If you can melt butter, you can make these cakes. Be brave and pull them out of the oven while they're still squidgy in the middle, for a dense, fudgy, heavenly treat.

Heat the oven to 180°C/Gas 4. Roughly chop the chocolate. Fit a heatproof bowl over a saucepan of simmering water, and combine the chocolate, sugar and butter in the bowl. Stir as it melts into a smooth, glossy sauce. Remove from heat and cool for 5 minutes.

Add the ground almonds and stir well. Beat in the egg yolks, one by one, until well mixed.

MAKES 12

200g dark, bitter chocolate

100g caster sugar

120g butter

100g ground almonds

4 eggs, separated

icing sugar for dusting

Place the egg whites in a large dry bowl and beat until stiff and peaky. Stir a large spoonful of egg white into the chocolate mixture to lighten it, then gently fold in the remaining egg white.

Spoon the mixture into lightly buttered large muffin moulds, or a 12-hole muffin tray lined with doubled muffin paper cases, and bake for 25 to 30 minutes.

Leave to cool for 10 minutes before removing from the moulds. Serve at room temperature, dusted with icing sugar, or store in an airtight tin for up to 3 days.

Caramel yoghurt

How easy is this? Combine rich Greek yoghurt with whipped cream, sprinkle with brown sugar, place in the fridge and you have a luscious caramel-topped creamy treat an hour later.

Whip the cream in a bowl until peaky. Lightly fold in the Greek yoghurt, using a spatula or large spoon, then pour into a wide, shallow bowl.

Scatter the soft brown sugar evenly over the surface. Cover and chill for 1 hour, until the sugar melts to form a caramel syrup.

When ready to serve, swirl the caramel sauce through the yoghurt. Serve with poached fruits, pies and tarts, chocolate cake, or as you would any rich cream.

SERVES 4
200ml whipping cream
200g thick Greek yoghurt
3 tbsp soft dark brown sugar

my friend the friand

anytime shortbread

My friend the friand

The friand is a truly awesome small, moist, dense, rich, almondy cake. It's very, very French, and very, very chic.

Heat the oven to 200°C/Gas 6. Melt the butter and allow to cool, then use 1 tbsp to coat 10 muffin tin moulds or individual oval baking moulds measuring 5 x 10cm.

Sift the icing sugar and flour into a bowl, and mix in the ground almonds. Lightly beat the egg whites with a fork, then fold them into the dry ingredients. Add the cooled, melted butter and lemon rind, and mix well.

Three-quarters fill each mould with the mixture and bake on the middle shelf of the oven for 10 minutes. Turn the tray around, and bake for another 5 to 10 minutes, until the tops are golden and spring back to the touch.

Leave in the tins for 5 minutes, then gently unmould onto a wire tray and leave to cool. Dust the friands with icing sugar to serve, or store them in an airtight container for up to 3 days.

MAKES 10

180g butter (preferably
   unsalted)

200g icing sugar

60g plain flour, sifted

120g ground almonds

5 large free-range egg whites

1 tsp grated lemon or
   orange rind

icing sugar for dusting

Anytime shortbread

Free shortbread from the restrictively narrow timeframe of Christmas, and make it throughout the year. Hallelujah.

Heat the oven to 150°C/Gas 2. Combine the butter, icing sugar and sea salt in a food processor and whiz until smooth.

Sift in the flour and rice flour, then pulse off and on, scraping down the sides from time to time, until the mixture gathers into a ball. Knead for a minute or two until smooth, then cut into two, wrap in cling film and refrigerate for 30 minutes.

Turn onto a floured surface and pat or lightly roll out the dough until 1 cm thick. Cut into 4 cm rounds, using a biscuit cutter or the rim of a liqueur glass. Reshape the scraps and cut more rounds. Place on a baking tray and prick with a fork.

Bake on the middle shelf of the oven for 10 minutes, then turn the tray around and bake for another 5 to 10 minutes until touched with colour. Leave to cool on the tray. Store the shortbread in an airtight container for up to 2 weeks.

MAKES 30
150 g unsalted butter, soft
75 g icing sugar
pinch of sea salt
150 g plain flour
75 g rice flour or cornflour

index

conversions

volume

5 ml	1 teaspoon (tsp)
10 ml	1 dessertspoon (dsp)
15 ml	1 tablespoon (tbsp)
20 ml	1 Australian tablespoon
30 ml	1 fl oz
40 ml	$1^{1}/_{2}$ fl oz
55 ml	2 fl oz
70 ml	$2^{1}/_{2}$ fl oz
85 ml	3 fl oz
90 ml	$3^{1}/_{2}$ fl oz
100 ml	$3^{3}/_{4}$ fl oz
115 ml	4 fl oz
125 ml	$4^{1}/_{2}$ fl oz
140 ml	5 fl oz
155 ml	$5^{1}/_{2}$ fl oz
170 ml	6 fl oz
185 ml	$6^{1}/_{2}$ fl oz
200 ml	7 fl oz
225 ml	8 fl oz
240 ml	$8^{1}/_{2}$ fl oz
255 ml	9 fl oz
285 ml	10 fl oz ($^{1}/_{2}$ pint)
350 ml	12 fl oz
375 ml	13 fl oz
400 ml	14 fl oz
425 ml	15 fl oz ($^{3}/_{4}$ pint)
450 ml	16 fl oz
565 ml	20 fl oz (1 pint)
710 ml	25 fl oz ($1^{1}/_{4}$ pints)
850 ml	30 fl oz ($1^{1}/_{2}$ pints)
1 litre	35 fl oz ($1^{3}/_{4}$ pints)
1.2 litres	2 pints

weight

7.5 g	$^{1}/_{4}$ oz
15 g	$^{1}/_{2}$ oz
20 g	$^{3}/_{4}$ oz
30 g	1 oz
40 g	$1^{1}/_{2}$ oz
55 g	2 oz
70 g	$2^{1}/_{2}$ oz
85 g	3 oz
90 g	$3^{1}/_{2}$ oz
115 g	4 oz
125 g	$4^{1}/_{2}$ oz
140 g	5 oz
170 g	6 oz
200 g	7 oz
225 g	8 oz
255 g	9 oz
285 g	10 oz
310 g	11 oz
340 g	12 oz
370 g	13 oz
400 g	14 oz
425 g	15 oz
455 g	1 lb
500 g	1 lb 2 oz
565 g	1 lb 4 oz
600 g	1 lb 5 oz
680 g	1 lb 8 oz
700 g	1 lb 9 oz
750 g	1 lb 10 oz
800 g	1 lb 12 oz
905 g	2 lb
1 kg	2 lb 3 oz

length

5 mm	$^{1}/_{4}$ inch
1 cm	$^{1}/_{2}$ inch
2.5 cm	1 inch
5 cm	2 inch
7.5 cm	3 inch
10 cm	4 inch
12 cm	5 inch
15 cm	6 inch
18 cm	7 inch
20 cm	8 inch
23 cm	9 inch
25 cm	10 inch
28 cm	11 inch
30 cm	12 inch

oven temperatures

140°C	275°F	Gas 1	Cool
150°C	300°F	Gas 2	Slow
170°C	325°F	Gas 3	Moderately slow
180°C	350°F	Gas 4	Moderate
200°C	400°F	Gas 6	Hot
220°C	425°F	Gas 7	Hot
230°C	450°F	Gas 8	Very hot